Can You Tell This Is a Knockoff?

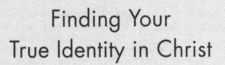

Finding Your True Identity in Christ

Missy Horsfall and Jocelyn Hamsher

BARBOUR
PUBLISHING

Print ISBN 978-1-61626-548-9

eBook Editions:
Adobe Digital Edition (.epub) 978-1-62029-024-8
Kindle and MobiPocket Edition (.prc) 978-1-62029-025-5

Published by Barbour Publishing, Inc., P.O. Box 719, Uhrichsville, Ohio 44683,
www.barbourbooks.com

*Our mission is to publish and distribute inspirational products offering exceptional value
and biblical encouragement to the masses.*

 Member of the
Evangelical Christian
Publishers Association

Printed in the United States of America.

This book is dedicated to every woman
who is searching and struggling to find her true
identity. Life can throw some tough stuff at us,
but we can know there's hope, there's healing,
there's joy, there's more. . .because there's
Jesus. Walk in truth my precious ones—
you're loved.

Jocelyn

This book is dedicated to my sisters,
Laura and Randi, along with my ever-increasing
circle of friends, who have touched my life
with their wisdom, love, and grace and have
taught me so much about who I really am.

Missy

To my Jesus, thank You for the life lessons found on the following pages. No matter how grueling the lesson, You don't let go. You are so patient and Your love for Your people overwhelms me. Thank You for Your unfathomable gift of grace, the power of Your Gospel, and Your inheritance You've shared with me. You have set my heart free! Oh, how I look forward to the dance. . .

To Bruce, the love of my life, there aren't enough words. You have lived out love, faith, and servant leadership in our home and spoken truth and encouragement to me for the past twenty-four years. After Jesus and His grace, God has given me no greater gift than you. I love you.

To Micah, Ty, and Cade, always remember. . .just because you're mine.

To Missy, your friendship is a gift, your partnership in ministry a blessing. Thank you for the privilege of writing with you.

Jocelyn

Jocelyn—I say with Paul, "I thank my God upon every remembrance of you." What a joy to call you friend.

Our deepest thanks are extended to those who shared their life stories with us—Tanya, Carrie, Sierra, Tammy, JoEllen, Hannah—and to Liz and Emily for their first draft reading and suggestions.

A special thanks to our agent Steve Laube and the wonderful folks at Barbour Publishing for their encouragement and support of Circle of Friends Ministries.

And for all my beautiful girls Beth, Lydia, Emily, Adalie, Isabel, and Clara—and the boys who love them well, J. T., Ryan, and Eric—you are the treasure of my heart.

Ned—I'll love you for always and forever.

Last, and most important, I bow in adoration to the One who created me and loves me beyond description. How grateful I am to be called Your own.

Missy

Contents

❖ ❖ ❖

Introduction

If someone asked, "Who are you?" how would you answer? Do you identify yourself by what you do, by what others think of you, or by how you feel? Or perhaps with your name, a description of yourself, or how many children you have? For some of us, finding out who we are can be a lifelong search, particularly if we believe our identity is found in who others tell us we are.

Women seem especially prone to believe how we look on the outside signifies who we are on the inside, as if our dress and appearance are the markers that portray our true identity. How misguided we can be when we determine who we are—or who others are—by the way we make ourselves appear.

Since bib overalls and a snap-up cowboy shirt was my favorite outfit in college, I'm not sure anyone should listen to me when it comes to fashion. However, even someone as couture-challenged as I am has heard of designers such as Dior, Calvin Klein, Ralph Lauren, Versace, Giorgio Armani, Yves Saint Laurent, or Coco Chanel. These famous names bring to mind gorgeous fabrics in rich colors draped with discreet but enormous price tags.

The dictionary defines a knockoff as a copy of something that sells for less than the original product. Usually this is an imitation of something popular or a well-known name in the fashion industry. More often than not it is inferior, a cheap copy of the original.

Now if you are like me, something like this would appeal to you because the original generally has that hefty price tag on it. It's going to cost me either what I don't have or what I think I can't afford. An imitation, a knockoff, will make it look like I own the real thing. So in reality, I would want a purse with a "Couch" label instead of "Coach" only because I might be able to fool someone into believing I had a more expensive handbag.

Let me say right up front that there is nothing wrong with imitation products, as long as you aren't trying to fool yourself into believing they are as good as the originals. I know many women who are great bargain hunters, and sometimes that includes finding a knockoff that closely resembles the genuine article without paying full price. However, as my friend Hannah learned, sometimes you get what you pay for.

Hannah and her best friend were in the big city hoping to take advantage of the opportunity to find some look-alike designer purses. Solicited by street vendors with the lure of designers like Fendi, Gucci, and Louis Vuitton, the girls found their way through busy streets and back alleys to buy their bargains. The shop owners tucked their purchases into black trash bags (it's illegal to sell imitations with similar designs or logos using brand names that are copyrighted). Throughout the day as they walked around, they saw hundreds of women carrying similar black bags. They seemed to look at each other in a way that said "You found fake handbags, too, huh?"

Hannah told me, "It was an experience I'll probably

always remember but not repeat. The thing about knockoffs is that they aren't the real quality things. All of mine are no longer usable; one has a bad zipper, and on another the strap popped. I've been paying full price ever since."

While this is an example of a lesson learned, I think it points to a deeper spiritual issue. When we settle for the imitation, we soon realize that it is not the real quality we are looking for, and we will end up like Hannah—paying full price because we settled for something less. Jesus Christ is the real thing—the authentic original. His enemy, Satan, is the counterfeit and often presents opportunities for us to grab on to a knockoff that may be appealing but will never be anything but an imitation.

Are you settling for a knockoff faith—one that gives the appearance of having it all together but accepts less than what God intended? God wants us to have the original! He never asks us to settle for less. Our identity—who we really are—is daughters of the King of kings who promises to provide our every need (see Philippians 4:19). We don't need to try to fake our spiritual fashion statement by trying to pretend to be something we are not.

Our prayer for you is that this book will lead you to uncover the freeing truth of who you are in Christ, but most importantly, that this journey will be one that will draw you closer to the One who created you. May God's Spirit speak to you through His Word in these next several chapters, expose lies that you have lived in, and bring you a fresh revelation of your true identity in Him.

CHAPTER ONE
Confident in Christ

It's in Christ that we find out who we are
and what we are living for. Long before we first
heard of Christ and got our hopes up, he had
his eye on us, had designs on us for glorious
living, part of the overall purpose he is
working out in everything and everyone.

It's in Christ that you, once you heard the
truth and believed it (this Message of your
salvation), found yourselves home free—
signed, sealed, and delivered by the Holy Spirit.
This signet from God is the first installment on what's
coming, a reminder that we'll get everything God has
planned for us, a praising and glorious life.

EPHESIANS 1:11–14 MSG

What could be more fun than a girls' getaway in New York City? A little pampering, a little sightseeing, and definitely shopping! Tammy and her friend JoEllen had the whole trip planned out, including staying at a five-star hotel where someone handed you a glass of champagne when you walked through the door. Everything went according to plan until they got to Chinatown. They had heard about great deals on knockoff purses that you could purchase there and, sure enough, a man approached them and handed them a card offering to show them where they could acquire a purse. The sidewalks were teeming with a mob of people on their way to and from, going about their busy lives. The gentleman didn't take them far; he unlocked a door right off the main street and then locked it again behind them. Tammy shifted her backpack and glanced at JoEllen, who gave her a reassuring smile. All would be well.

Following the man up a flight of stairs, Tammy saw a woman appear to one side of her. She stumbled and fell against Tammy's back. Immediately concerned about the woman's safety, Tammy leaned over to help her up and ask if she was all right. Yes, she assured her, she was fine. Tammy let her go, still concerned because the woman appeared to be homeless. The woman disappeared, and Tammy headed up the stairs to join her friend.

They entered a small room filled with all kinds of

13

purses. There were a few people shopping, and the two friends were soon looking for purchases to make as well. JoEllen noticed that Tammy's backpack was opened and—you guessed it—her wallet was missing. When Tammy exclaimed, "I've been robbed!" the salespeople in the room began to get excited and cried out, "Not by us! Not by us! You must go." The women were hustled down the stairs and led back out onto the street with the door locked behind them again. It seemed there was great fear that this illegal operation would be discovered, and the owners didn't want the police involved.

While Tammy wasn't carrying a lot of cash, she did have credit cards and, of course, her driver's license. With her identification missing, she was worried about being allowed to board the plane home. Finding who robbed her would be unlikely, but she needed to report the theft and try to get some identification to be able to get through airport security. When they got to the police station, a detective took her statement and began asking questions. "What's your name? Where were you when the robbery occurred?"

Uh-oh. Things had just gotten a little stickier than she had counted on. But Tammy is one of the most authentic, up-front people I know. She calmly began telling the officer exactly where they had been, while JoEllen looked at her wide-eyed from across the room. Could they be arrested for trying to buy illegal purses? Tammy is also a little naive. As she describes it, she and her husband don't even lock up their home in the small town they live in. So many people had approached the women wanting to sell them purses—didn't that make it "less" illegal? As the officer continued to gather information, Tammy confessed that she couldn't describe the person who robbed her; the chances of catching the woman—or man wearing a wig and heavy overcoat—were slim.

Her credit cards canceled and a faxed copy of her passport in hand, Tammy determined to enjoy what she could of her girls' getaway. The next day she and JoEllen were again shopping on the street and approached by a man who handed them a card and offered them purses for sale. This time they went through a regular storefront housing souvenirs to a back room full of knockoff Coach, Dolce and Gabbana, and other designer purses. . .

Armed with their purchases and wiser for their experiences, they found their adventures were just beginning when they arrived at the airport early to catch their flight home. With no ID, even the police report and copy of her passport were not enough to allow Tammy past security. Held for over an hour, she had to answer questions from the security officers. Mother's maiden name? Father's middle name? The routine questions became complicated when she tried to explain that her husband went by a nickname derived from his middle name and that his professional name that was on all their legal documents was actually an initial, not his given name! As the officials checked their database of information, they questioned whether she was who she claimed to be. It took some time, but they finally allowed her to get through the heightened security measures.

Whether it's providing our driver's license or other

documents when we travel to prove we are whom we say we are, or introducing ourselves to someone we've just met, our names are an important part of defining our identities.

Do you like your name? Our names can become symbols of who we are, whether they started out as a namesake (I'm named after my great-grandmother and her sister), meaningful because of an event or circumstance (consider the boy who was named Wrigley Fields after the baseball field!), or just because our parents liked the sound of it. In some cultures, it is considered bad luck to name a baby before he or she is born. In our culture, the months leading up to a child's birth can be taken up by the great debate of what to name him or her. Here are a few names that should have been contemplated just a little while longer:

- Armand Hammer
- Will Power
- Candi Barr
- Peter Abbott
- Robin Banks
- Tim Burr
- Zack Lee Wright
- Thurston Unger
- Paige Turner

Or consider these choices: A popular actress on the TV show *Without a Trace*, Poppy Montgomery's real name is Poppy Petal Emma Elizabeth Deveraux Donahue. Her brother's name is Jethro Tull, and her sisters are Rosie Thorn, Daisy Yellow, Lily Belle, and Marigold Sun. There's also Tu Morrow, daughter of actor Rob Morrow, and Ima Hogg, daughter of Texas Governor James Stephen Hogg. Or how about Anthony Philip David Terry Frank Donald Stanley Gerry Gordon Stephen James Oatway. He's named after the Queens Park Rangers, a professional English football club. No wonder they call him Charlie! Consider if you were one of musician Frank Zappa's kids—Moon Unit, Dweezil, Ahmet Emuukha Rodan, or Diva Thin Muffin Pigeen.

Feeling a little better about your own name? Chances are it's not as unusual as the ones I've just listed, but maybe you've picked up a name along the way that no more suits you than one of these, an "emotional name" that you have come to believe is true about yourself. Are you wearing a name that isn't yours, such as Abandoned or Unlovable, or perhaps Stupid or Inadequate?

If we define ourselves by what other people say about us, we are mistaken. We need to define ourselves by what the One who made us says of us. You can interpret a painting, but only the artist can tell you what he was thinking or feeling and what he intended the painting to mean. We were created by God as a unique expression of Himself. Only He can define us and tell us who we are.

Ephesians 1:4 says that He chose us in Christ before the foundations of the world. Before time began, God planned on calling you His own and adopting you into His family. He has a name for you:

His child (John 1:12)

His friend (John 15:15)

A new creation (2 Corinthians 5:17)

Righteous and holy (Ephesians 4:24)

God's workmanship—His handiwork (Ephesians
      2:10)

A saint (1 Corinthians 1:2)

A joint heir with Christ (Romans 8:17)

Elect of God, Chosen and Beloved (Colossians
      3:12, Ephesians 1:11, John 15:16,
      1 Peter 2:9 NIV)

Accepted (Romans 15:7)

Anointed (1 John 2:27)

Gifted (Romans 12:6)

Beautiful (Isaiah 52:7)

Redeemed (Galatians 3:13)

Ephesians 2 goes on to compare who we were before we knew Christ with who we are after we have a relationship with Him. Look at the contrast!

We Were:	*We Are:*
Dead in our sins (v. 1)	Made alive in Him (v. 5)
Under Satan's control (vv. 2, 3)	Saved through faith (v. 8)
Outside the promises of God (v. 12)	Now the temple of God (v. 22)
Aliens and strangers (v. 12)	Fellow citizens (v. 19)

Far off from God (v. 13)	Brought near to God (v. 13)
Enemies of God (v. 15)	At peace with God (v. 15)
Without hope (v. 12)	Greatly loved by God (v. 4)

And that's just the beginning! Because Christ was the sinless Son of God, I have been forgiven (Colossians 1:14). Because He was rejected, I have been accepted (Ephesians 1:5–6). Because He was crucified, I now have eternal life (Romans 6:23). Because Jesus rose from the dead, I am now seated with Him in the heavenly places (Ephesians 2:6).

When we define ourselves by what the world says or by others' expectations of us, we come to the wrong conclusion about ourselves. God is the one who made us, and it is God who reveals our identity to us. Psalm 139 tells us that He knows us intimately and formed us in our mother's womb, but even before that our story was written in His book (v. 16)—*before* we were created He knew us and loved us.

How do you define who you are?

My father was a career military man, and when he retired I was just going into seventh grade. We moved home from overseas and settled in my parents' hometown, so I went to school with many of my cousins. In fact, I rode the school bus with them. I was so excited to be on the bus with the "big kids"—the high schoolers who sat in the back seats of the bus. One day I overheard one of them saying he was Catholic, and another student said she was Lutheran. All of a sudden they turned to me and asked, "What are you, Missy?" I was thrilled to be included in the conversation, and I proudly announced, "I'm a prostitute!" I wasn't sure what was so funny or why they laughed at what I said (someone had to explain it to me later that the word I meant was *Protestant*), but I knew that what I had said was terribly wrong and not at all what I meant to communicate about who I was.

I've continued to struggle through the years trying to define myself. As a pastor's wife I found myself developing the ability to wear a mask. I didn't play the piano, didn't sing, and often felt isolated from the women in my church and the need to keep a distance because of the expectations I perceived were coming from the church body. Notice I said, *perceived*. I found I could hide pretty well behind this mask of being the perfect pastor's wife—smile, say all the right words, and attend all the activities and ministries of the church. Afraid to show my real self, I got used to pretending that everything was okay. My deepest struggles remained hidden. I defined myself by my role as pastor's wife. Have you done that? Defined yourself by what you *do* rather than by *who you are*?

There was a period of time when my husband was not in the pastorate, and I began to see just how much this name—this identity of pastor's wife—meant to me. I used it to define who I was, and it gave me significance. I realized that I needed to focus on who I was rather than what I did. I think this developed in my life at an early age. I found being known as the Colonel's daughter a way of reassuring myself I had worth. While I am proud to be my father's daughter, it is not this relationship that gives me

Can You Tell This Is a Knockoff?

significance. My self-worth wavered on what other people thought of me, which continued into my adult years. But who I am is not defined by what I do or my relationship with others.

Except for one—and that is my relationship to Jesus Christ.

Jesus came for that purpose—to make a way for a relationship with God. On our own merit we can't approach God, but with Christ's sacrifice for our sin we accept His righteousness as our own (2 Corinthians 5:21; Romans 3:21–26). This exchange seals our relationship with our Heavenly Father.

Our security is found in Christ. It is because of who He is that we can rest assured in who we will become. "He who began a good work in you will carry it on to completion until the day of Christ Jesus" (Philippians 1:6 NIV). His transforming power begins with our confession of faith in Him and continues until we are reunited with Him in heaven. We become a new creation, becoming more and more what He planned and designed for us to be.

Adopted into God's family and sealed by His Spirit, we find our identity in *Christ*. This is our eternal surety. This is the rock and foundation we stand on. There is great freedom in knowing that who we are is not dependent on us. The One who cannot be shaken and who never changes secures our identity.

My friend and her husband became foster parents for a very young boy who came out of a chaotic and destructive home. Even at his young age, he knew the difference between the two living situations. As time passed, my friends were able to eventually adopt this little guy. He was so excited to have his name changed! However, he worried if it would really happen and if he truly would be a "Smith" now. His new parents copied his adoption certificate and shrank it to the size of a business card and had it laminated. The boy carried it around to show everyone he had a new identity and to remind himself that he was part of a new family.

John the Baptist was a man who knew who he was. Before he was born, the angel Gabriel foretold his birth:

> When Zechariah saw him, he was startled and was gripped with fear. But the angel said to him: "Do not be afraid, Zechariah; your prayer has been heard. Your wife Elizabeth will bear you a son, and you are to call him John. He will be a joy and delight to you, and many will rejoice because of his birth, for he will be great in the sight of the Lord. He is never to take wine or other fermented drink, and he will be filled with the Holy Spirit even before he is born. He will bring back many of the people of Israel to the Lord their God. And he will go on before the Lord, in the spirit and power of Elijah, to turn the hearts of the parents to their children and the disobedient to the wisdom of the righteous — to make ready a people prepared for the Lord." (Luke 1:12–17 NIV)

Can you imagine it? From the time he was old enough to understand, his parents were telling him the story of his birth. His parents were "very old" and had no children.

God did the miraculous, and Elizabeth conceived. This little boy knew from the beginning of his life that he was very special. There was great celebration at his birth, because it was clear from the start that he was set apart by God to do great things. His father Zechariah had become mute because he couldn't believe what the angel was telling him. When John was born everyone thought he would be named after his father, but Elizabeth said no, and Zechariah confirmed it by writing on a tablet: "His name is John." The importance of who he was, and what God intended for him to do with his life, was planned long before the foundation of the world. What we so often forget is that this is true for us as well!

Psalm 139:16–17 (NIV) says, "Your eyes saw my unformed body; all the days ordained for me were written in your book before one of them came to be. How precious to me are your thoughts, God! How vast is the sum of them!" It's probably true that your parents weren't visited by an angel and told what to name you—but surely God knew who you were. He planned your life from the beginning, and the same way He had a purpose for John the Baptist to fulfill, He has one for you, too.

When I think about John the Baptist, I imagine a man who was so secure in who he was that other people's opinions rolled right off his back. I don't think he struggled with pleasing others or worrying about what someone else would say. Look at his lifestyle—he hung out in the wilderness dressed in camel hair, eating locusts and wild honey. He was as far from conforming to society and his culture as any hippie in the sixties. He was so focused on being whom the Lord called him and made him to be that he didn't have time to be swayed to consider anything else.

And what was his focus? In Mark 1, the writer tells us that the prophet Isaiah talked about John years before he was born. John was a messenger, and his purpose was to prepare the way for the Messiah, Jesus. He called people to repentance and pointed them to the Savior. John knew who he was in Christ. His surety and security was in knowing who Christ was and understanding his own role in helping others come to know Jesus as well.

John's message was "Repent of your sins and turn to God, for the Kingdom of Heaven is near" (Matthew 3:2 NLT). The people thought John might be the Messiah, but he told them there was One coming that was greater—that John was unworthy to even be His slave and untie the straps of His sandals. John even objected to baptizing Jesus and agreed only when Jesus pointed out that it was important to carry out all God required.

For me, John's security in who he was and what he was created to do is shown clearly in the fact that he was Jesus' cousin. They were family; they grew up together, knew all the family quirks and stories. Perhaps it would have been easy for John to think, I'm the oldest. Who does He think He is, usurping my position of seniority? But there was no jealousy on John's part because he had a clear picture of his own identity.

Can you and I say the same thing?

While we can look at John the Baptist and see from the rest of the story in scripture that God had a distinct purpose for his life—don't miss out on this truth: God has

Can You Tell This Is a Knockoff?

created you and I with the same kind of uniqueness and purpose. Like John, our identity is found in Christ, and we need to look to Him as the ultimate example. Jesus knew who He was and what his Father had called Him to do. Because of that, He loved and lived unconditionally, sacrificially, and with great boldness. He was able to live in the freedom His Father gave Him, find protection from Satan's schemes, and walk in obedience—all the while extending the good news of salvation and deliverance, even while facing the cross to come.

Jesus was and is in the transformation business—He transforms lives, hearts, and even names. He renamed Jacob, meaning "deceiver," to Israel, meaning, "God heals." God called Sarai, meaning "princess," the new name of Sarah. Sarah has the same meaning, but God added to her the blessing of being the mother of nations and kings and to be used by God for His purposes. Jesus stepped in and renamed Simon, meaning "flat-nosed," to Peter, meaning, "rock."

Have you attempted to walk in names that don't fit? We have been given names that we were never meant to answer to. We have named ourselves out of our own longing to find a place to belong, to fit in, to feel accepted. But the good news is Jesus has come to transform our names as well. God Himself gave us a name (Revelation 2:17), one that He has been calling us since He knew us as His own. And it's time we start answering to it.

In Isaiah 61 it says the spiritually and physically needy He has renamed the spiritually and emotionally rich. He has renamed the brokenhearted as healed. He has called the prisoner delivered, and those who are lost, He has called restored. No matter what our situation—coming from a family of divorce, being rejected or abandoned, never feeling like we are good enough, loneliness, juggling life unsuccessfully—we all have been given a new name in Christ. We can be confident in Him!

Can You Tell This Is a Knockoff?

Discussion Questions

1. List the names you have adopted for yourself that are untrue. ....
   ....
   ....

2. Write Psalm 149:4 below:
   ....
   ....

3. Read John 17:20–23. How does God love you (v. 23)? How does it make you feel to know that God loves you just as much as He loves His own Son, Jesus Christ?
   ....
   ....

4. Read 1 Peter 2:9–10 and contrast your past with your present. ....
   ....
   ....

5. What is the ongoing theme in the following verses?
   • Micah 7:18 ....
   • Deuteronomy 10:15 ....

- Job 33:26 ....
- Psalm 37:23 ....
- Proverbs 11:20 ....
- Proverbs 15:8 ....

6. Complete this sentence according to the verses below:

"I am. . ."

....

Ephesians 1:5; Galatians 4:5

....

....

John 15:15; James 2:23

....

....

1 Corinthians 6:17

....

....

Colossians 2:10

....

....

John 15:19

....

....

Notes:

....
....
....
....
....
....
....
....
....
....
....
....
....
....
....
....
....
....
....
....
....
....
....
....

CHAPTER TWO
Secure to Serve

Agree with each other, love each other, be deep-spirited friends. Don't push your way to the front; don't sweet-talk your way to the top. Put yourself aside, and help others get ahead. Don't be obsessed with getting your own advantage. Forget yourselves long enough to lend a helping hand. . . . Go out into the world uncorrupted, a breath of fresh air in this squalid and polluted society. Provide people with a glimpse of good living and of the living God.

PHILIPPIANS 2:1–4, 15 MSG

My husband and I were walking out of the grocery store when we passed a man and his wife, standing by their car with the trunk open. As the woman stood to the side watching, utterly silent, the man attempted to push a child's blue plastic swimming pool into the trunk. With only three feet sunk into the trunk and obviously not budging any farther, another five feet stuck up into the air. Struggling, the man muttered emphatically, "Nobody's gonna call me a fool!"

Without looking at each other, my husband and I began giggling, knowing the other one's thoughts. It was obvious that this man had assured his wife the pool would fit, and now full of pride, he didn't want to admit his mistake. Oh, how often we've all been there.

Isn't it amazing how quickly the sin of pride can get the best of us? We will do lots of things to defend ourselves so we don't look silly or just plain wrong. What's so ironic about the whole thing is that what we are attempting to avoid—looking stupid—happens anyway because of our pride. We will justify or make excuses, get angry and defensive, make sure we slip into the conversation how we were instrumental in the success of a project, or put down others to make ourselves feel better. Have you ever been with a friend trying to share your heart's concerns or life issues and she continues to turn the conversation back to herself? In fact, by nature we will do whatever it takes to serve ourselves and make sure we come out unscathed, looking good, and on top in every situation.

Starting in grade school, I discovered something about myself—I had a competitive spirit. Whether it was a sporting event or a friendly board game, I wanted to win. I wanted to be the best, be noticed, and frankly, be better than everybody else at what I did. And when I didn't win or wasn't the best, I pouted. I became angry, critical of myself, and jealous of others. Now, being young, my emotional immaturity was somewhat normal and not surprising. However, as I grew up, emotionally I was stuck. My pride was a cover for my fear—fear of failing, fear of getting hurt, fear of being insignificant. "Protect self at all costs" became my mantra.

Now instead of competing with others in a game, I was subconsciously competing with others in life. To promote someone else and put myself aside was foreign and, in my mind, suicide. Because I was so insecure, to genuinely be able to celebrate with another person when he or she succeeded was difficult. If the achievement was something that didn't concern me, I was happy for the person. But if it was someone who had a similar gifting as mine or experienced what I desired, I was jealous. I would say encouraging things, but to say I meant it with joy would be a lie—because in my mind, another's success meant my failure.

I didn't want it to be this way; my desire was to serve the Lord and see Him glorified. But when I felt threatened or overlooked, when my "kingdom" was seemingly under

Can You Tell This Is a Knockoff?

attack, I saw the ugly and sinful core of my being rise up for what it was—self-serving and self-glorifying. I have listened to others' struggles, watched others compare, compete, and jockey for position in the Body of Christ. I have witnessed churches become territorial of their people and programs and become islands. I knew that I wasn't alone—the god of self, fear, and insecurity sits on the throne of hearts everywhere.

It's a journey, but through God's patient, gentle, and persistent ways, He grows us by revealing the truth of Himself. When we discover our identity in Jesus, we can see the lie we have believed for so long. Learning more about the heart of God, who He is, and who we are because of Jesus, opens the eyes of our hearts like never before. Jesus Christ is the Chosen One, and He has set us free—free from ourselves, from the lies that ensnare us, from sin's control—and placed us on a path to embrace a new way of thinking and living. But the choice to believe it is ours.

God spoke about Jesus through Isaiah saying,

Take a good look at my servant. I'm backing him to the hilt. He's the one I chose, and I couldn't be more pleased with him. I've bathed him with my Spirit, my life. He'll set everything right among the nations. He won't call attention to what he does with loud speeches or gaudy parades. He won't brush aside the bruised and the hurt and he won't disregard the small and insignificant, but he'll steadily and firmly set things right. He won't tire out and quit. He won't be stopped until he's

finished his work—to set things right on earth. . . .
I have set you [Jesus] among my people to bind
them to me, and provided you as a lighthouse to
the nations, to make a start at bringing people
into the open, into light: opening blind eyes,
releasing prisoners from dungeons, emptying the
dark prisons. I am God. That's my name. (Isaiah
42:1–4, 6–8 MSG)

Because of Jesus, we can finally live in security. The
identity we once answered to of "overlooked, forgotten,
or unwanted" has been destroyed. Unfortunately, we can
choose to still wear it because we often allow our feelings
to become truth. But the truth is Jesus was chosen by
God, and if we have a relationship with Him, so are you and
I. Because we are hidden in Christ, our security is wrapped,
rooted, anchored, and saturated in the constant, never-
changing, and irrevocable "chosenness" of Jesus Christ.
Jesus tells His disciples, which includes you and me, that
we don't belong to the world but have been chosen out of
it; that we have been appointed to go and bear fruit that
won't spoil (John 15:16, 19). He relays through His disciple
Peter that those who follow Jesus have been chosen by
God and are precious to Him (1 Peter 2:4) and that we
have a high calling. He declares His "chosen to be a holy
people, God's instruments to do his work and speak out
for him, to tell others of the night-and-day difference he
made for [us]—from nothing to something, from rejected to
accepted" (1 Peter 2:9–10, MSG).

We get stuck in the rut of the way this broken world

thinks rather than keeping our hearts and minds in tune with God. In our world when someone is chosen for something, that means others are not. Our thoughts immediately go back to physical education class, when we waited our turn to be chosen next for the basketball team. As more and more people left the line to join a team, our self-esteem left as well. To not be chosen first or even second may lead us to feel insignificant, less than, or rejected. So the thought of bringing promotion to others leads us to think we'll lose our position of security or importance. We protect our hearts from hurt and react by withdrawing, lashing out, or hosting an insidious jealousy. In this case, our security isn't rooted in the identity of Jesus, which He wrapped us in, or His immovable completeness but in our self-effort, wavering abilities, and unstable emotions.

Years ago, a woman came into my life of whom I was a bit leery. I knew she had become a believer, but to my insecure heart, I wasn't comfortable with the ties she had to my family. However, the Lord wanted to do a work and set out ever so gently (but seemingly pushy at the time) to accomplish it. He kept bringing her name to me through people I would run into throughout the community. At that time, I was my church's director of women's ministry and led an annual community women's retreat. I was always looking for women who had testimonies to share about what God was doing in their lives. This woman's name was suggested more than once from unsuspecting and well-meaning ladies. Of all people to run into, I even met a woman at a community garage sale who introduced herself as this woman's mother-in-law!

Unbelievably, this woman went from moving into town to having a son who just happened to be in my son's class. It didn't end there—our sons became good friends. I knew God was nudging me to ask her to share at the next women's event, and everything within me recoiled and resisted—until finally, I had no choice. I called her and asked her to breakfast for the following week. We met and talked for two hours. We had tons in common—similar personalities, backgrounds, perspectives, struggles, and concerns. The time flew, and before we parted ways, I asked her if she would be willing to share her powerful testimony of how the Lord had worked in her life. With tears filling her eyes, she confessed her fear about doing that but also her heart of sincerity, as she had recently told the Lord she would share her story if He asked her.

It was truly incredible. She shared at our next women's event, and the Holy Spirit revealed Himself and touched many through her witness of His greatness. A woman I once held at arms length, I now called friend and sister. My ugly heart transformed, her faith encouraged, a relationship birthed, a body of believers impacted, our God glorified. I learned that as I reached out and gave, I didn't lose. I gained joy, contentment, a peace in knowing that I had obeyed, and a genuine sense of unity. My security didn't lessen but was only affirmed. There is joy in giving opportunity, in encouraging, in surrendering and stepping out of the way so God can do only what God can do.

When we're anchored in the identity and security Jesus offers, we can rejoice with, encourage, affirm, lift up, serve, pray for, pour into, and cheer for others and truly mean it because being chosen by God means that He will never forget us, leave us out, or leave us behind. Being chosen means God has entrusted us with a significant purpose and calling, no matter where we are in life. Even in the trials and disappointments, He is still choosing and using us right where we are to declare His faithfulness. When we embrace and plug into Jesus' "chosenness," we can see others with different eyes—how God sees them. They are no longer threats or competitors, no longer superior or inferior, but chosen vessels that God delights in, traveling the specific path God has called them to for His glory. Their success does not mean our failure; their blessing does not mean our curse. Their giftedness does not mean our lack. In fact, all God has is ours (Luke 15:31)! He has given each of us *all* that we need! We are complete in Jesus Christ. He fills us up with Himself. In 1 Corinthians 4, the people were comparing Paul and Apollos so Paul responded to them with this truth:

> *Isn't everything you have and everything you are sheer gifts from God? So what's the point of all this comparing and competing? You already have all you need. You already have more access to God than you can handle. Without bringing either Apollos or me into it, you're sitting on top of the world—at least God's world—and we're right there, sitting alongside you!* (1 Corinthians 4:7–8 MSG)

It's not our kingdom; it's His. There is no room for our petty competition or rivalry. We have been chosen not so *we* may be elevated, but so *Jesus* is. We are not working against others but *with* others to exalt our King. He blesses us with spiritual gifts not for our benefit but to energize the body. It's His life-saving message, and we are privileged and humbled ambassadors to be able to deliver it. When we jockey for position or compete with others in any way, we attempt to take center stage, a place we weren't made for and don't belong in. Our encouragement of another doesn't take away from us but only promotes Him! As we add value to others and love them well, our Heavenly Father is praised and glorified. His church is unified. Our high calling is to declare Jesus Christ to the world. It is our lives that declare His praise, that witness to the world and draw them to see and glorify God.

How does this identity of "chosen" look? It looks like a life that Jesus is living in and through—a life of humility and servanthood.

Picture the scene in John 13. Jesus and His disciples are sitting around the table, towel and pitcher nearby, but no one makes a move toward it. Washing feet was reserved for the lowest, most menial of servants, and quite frankly the disciples didn't feel they fit the bill. However, there is One who does stand and reach for the pitcher. Jesus, King of kings, removes His outer clothing and wraps a towel around His waist. God, on His knees, pours water into a basin and moves around the table to serve each of His disciples.

As He washes away the dirt from His disciples' feet

this night, the next night will ensure the washing of filth from their hearts. He scrubs the feet of every one of them, even Judas, His betrayer. Knowing just hours away awaits the kiss of betrayal, fleeing friends, and agonizing death, Jesus focuses on teaching His disciples what true love looks like—servanthood. How could He do it? How could He be focusing on others at a time like this? They should be the ones doting on Him, listening to His fears and concerns, supporting Him, encouraging Him with the promises of God, and praying for Him. But Jesus realizes His time is short, and His disciples need not only a life lesson but also a lifestyle. Knowing who He is, whose He is, and where He's returning, He bends His knees with confident resolve, the deepest humility, and a love within His heart worth dying for. He knew what He was called to do—to carry out the work His Father had given Him and to take care of the ones His Father had entrusted to Him.

When Jesus took off His robe of royalty and put on His "apron" (John 13:3–6 MSG) of humility, He remained wrapped in the security of His "chosenness," His Father's love and faithfulness. With the robe comes the apron.

When he had finished washing their feet, he put on his clothes and returned to his place. "Do you understand what I have done for you?. . .You call me 'Teacher' and 'Lord,' and rightly so, for that is what I am. Now that I, your Lord and Teacher, have washed your feet, you also should wash one another's feet. I have set you an example that you should do as I have done for you. Very truly

I tell you, no servant is greater than his master, nor is a messenger greater than the one who sent him. Now that you know these things, you will be blessed if you do them." (John 13:12–17 NIV)

Do we know who we are, whose we are, and where we're headed? Does the identity that we have chosen to anchor into allow us to serve with freedom, security, humility, joy, peace, and a genuine desire to obey? If not, then we're not anchored to the Rock. But we can be. As followers and servants of Jesus, we are undeservedly privileged to wear the royal robe. There's no threat in laying it down to put on the apron. Because when Jesus took his last breath and cried out on the cross, "It is finished," God came to us who were in line and destined for the losing team, looked us square in the eye, and said, "I choose you."

This "chosenness" came alive to me when I had the privilege of attending an adoption hearing for a beautiful young woman. Her friends and family sat in the courtroom bubbling over with excitement and yet trying to be quiet. Sierra was in the next room and had no idea today was the day she was going to be adopted by Carrie, her stepmother of three years. However, it wasn't a typical adoption. Sierra was an adult—eighteen years old and ready to head into the armed services. This adoption, even though atypical, was every bit as precious as one that would take place for a young child. You see, Sierra had a father, but her birth mother had left her when Sierra was just five years old. When she was eight, her mother told her she didn't want to see her anymore or have anything to do with her. Sierra had grown up without knowing and experiencing her mother's love and acceptance.

As Sierra entered the courtroom, she was obviously curious as to why all of her friends and family were there. (Carrie had come up with a fabulous cover story.) Her stepmother approached Sierra, extending a bracelet. "Sierra, today would you allow me to adopt you? Would you become my daughter? Would you allow me to become your mother?"

I will never forget what happened next. Sierra jumped up out of her seat and placed both hands over her face. With tears flowing down her cheeks, she fell into Carrie's arms and cried. They hugged for several minutes, and when Sierra stepped back she looked at her stepmother and said, "I finally have a mom."

For whatever reason, one mother chose to walk away and reject Sierra both in word and action. But Carrie came into her life and not only chose to stay, but by her actions she also demonstrated that she chose *Sierra*. "Would you be my daughter?"—words of healing applied to a festering wound opened years earlier. Carrie chose to love Sierra, serve her, pray for her, encourage her, speak truth to her, listen to her, be her mother, and be her friend. She chose to put on the apron of humility to be one of the most important persons in Sierra's life. Because no matter how old we are, there is something priceless about knowing where we belong and whose we are that provides the security we need to face the world.

Jesus has chosen you specifically, and today He

asks you, "Would you be mine?" With the acceptance of that invitation, you can fall into His arms and rest in the security that He is. God provided security for Jesus as He stooped in submission; He provides it for you and me as we bend our knee to serve and lift up others.

Jesus sacrificially and lovingly submitted to serve us because He trusted His Father and was secure in His love. But He was also willing to serve, love, and lay down His life because He carried the essence of God Himself (Hebrews 1:3).

My teenage son, Ty, is a "coach" through and through. When he sets a goal for himself, he is disciplined and committed to reach it, no matter what it is. He works hard and puts the time in, and because of that, he sees results. Because he is wired with leadership ability, he motivates others to set goals and follow through. When he heard me talking about working out, he felt compelled to create a plan for me for the next two months. He would ask me every day if I had done my workout, giving me an encouraging word if I had followed through.

One evening after it was already dark outside, I sat in the kitchen talking to Ty as he finished doing the dishes. As usual he asked if I had worked out that day. I sheepishly responded with a "No." He asked me what my reasons were, and with each one I gave, he shot it down with truth. "No excuses" was his motto. Commitment was in order, despite the hour of the day, the weather, or my emotional state. There was a goal to be reached, a bigger picture to be realized. I had to chuckle as I sat there, a thirty-nine-year-old woman, being held accountable by a thirteen-year-old young man, who was absolutely right. He was young, but the next words out of his mouth were wise and spoken from the true heart of a leader: "Mom, get your shoes on. I'm doing it with you." And so we did. I ran that night better than any other time before.

In a much greater way, we have our Coach, our Leader, the Spirit and essence of our Savior within us. He not only came up with the plan and the purpose for our lives, saying, "Go, do it," but He also says, "Get your shoes on. I'm doing it with you."

God's heart is one of passion and justice, and it is one of gentleness and humility. Jesus took off His robe and grabbed a towel for His disciples that day in the upper room, but when He lay on the cross, He took off His robe and grabbed a towel for you and me. Where we once felt threatened to lift up others and help them get ahead, we can now live in security. We serve with joy because we are chosen through Jesus, because we have found a place to belong with God, because we know where we're going. We serve freely because our God does. We serve in love, because God lives *in* us and we live *in* Him. We can't do it in our own strength, but He can. How abundant our lives can be because He gave us His! Every day we can choose to rest in His divine life living in and through us. Take heart, there's hope of change. Because of Jesus in us, we can choose serving others over serving self—and love it!

Over the next several months, spend time in prayer talking to Jesus about your security in Him and how it relates to serving others. Ask the Holy Spirit for His help and revelation in showing you who He is and who you are in Him. As He gives you opportunity (which He will), step out in faith and practice being other-centered. Prayerfully choose two people with whom you can serve and begin to encourage intentionally.

Perhaps that begins by inviting a friend to coffee or intentionality in engaging someone who seems to be isolated and doing life alone. Maybe that's making yourself available to a younger woman for mentoring. Perhaps that's coming alongside an individual who is experiencing the same struggle you have previously worked through. Maybe it means stepping out in your security in Jesus and establishing a relationship with someone you have been jealous of, intimidated by, or sensed as a threat to your position or role. The opportunity may begin right in your own home—seeing the strengths in your spouse or children and building them up. In this greater level of living in Christ, know you are secure to serve. This freedom and joy to give to and encourage others without fear is yours. Jesus died to give it to you. You no longer have to wear the knockoff identity of "overlooked." You've been given an identity that is genuine. You, my friend, have been chosen.

Discussion Questions

1. How can you personally resonate with the struggle of serving self over serving others? Have you ever felt threatened or fearful to encourage or invest in other people, to help others succeed? Conversely, have you failed to reach out and serve those you may have looked down upon? ....

    ....

    ....

2. Reread the passage from Isaiah 42:1–4, 6–8. Just from these few verses, discuss the character and heart of Jesus—who He is, what He does, and what He doesn't do. Now read Isaiah 49:14–16. How do all these verses speak to you personally? ....

    ....

    ....

3. Your identity in Christ brings a new and true perspective. What does being chosen mean to you? Does this truth replace any lies you may have believed about your identity? ....

    ....

    ....

4. Think of those you may be intimidated by, compare yourself to, or be slow to encourage. How can your "chosenness" affect the way you see them? How does *their* "chosenness" affect the way you see them? ....

....

....

5. Looking at the heart of Jesus for you and knowing that His divine, abundant life lives in and through you, how does this provide rest and security for you to serve, invest in, and encourage freely? ....

....

....

6. How does encouraging and serving one another impact unity in the Body of Christ? Growing the Body of Christ? How can our insecurity hinder unity and "growing up" others in the faith?...................................

....

....

7. "You know that the rulers of the Gentiles lord it over them, and their high officials exercise authority over them. Not so with you. Instead, whoever wants to become great among you must be your servant, and whoever wants to be first must be your slave—just as the Son of Man did not come to be served, but

to serve, and to give his life as a ransom for many"
(Matthew 20:25–28 NIV).

Name two people you will be intentional with over the
next several months. How do you plan to do that?.......
....
....

8. How have you experienced Proverbs 11:25 in your
own life?...
....
....

Notes:

CHAPTER THREE
Gifted by Grace

Living then, as every one of you does, in pure grace, it's important that you not misinterpret yourselves as people who are bringing this goodness to God. No, God brings it all to you. The only accurate way to understand ourselves is by what God is and by what he does for us, not by what we are and what we do for him. In this way we are like the various parts of a human body. Each part gets its meaning from the body as a whole, not the other way around. The body we're talking about is Christ's body of chosen people.

ROMANS 12:3–5 MSG

Have you ever been confused about who you are based on where you belong? My husband is a bivocational pastor, and to support our family he drives for a transport company and delivers vehicles across the country. His schedule varies daily, and he will often end up far from home on overnight trips and will rely on the kindness of relatives and friends for lodging.

On a long haul to Florida, he made arrangements to spend the night with a couple he has stayed with on several occasions. He arrived in the early evening and noted that Sam's car was in the drive. He patted the dog lying on their porch and knocked on the door. No one answered, but the door was open, and since this couple are close friends of ours and they were expecting him, he let himself in. He dropped his bag and noted the blanket folded neatly on the end of the couch. He slipped off his boots and went to get a drink of water. As he passed the kitchen counter he noted several school papers on the counter and drawings on the refrigerator. Sam and Susan's son is grown, and they have no grandchildren, so my husband took a closer look at his surroundings. He'd made himself comfortable in someone else's home! It didn't take him long to grab his bag and boots and flee from the house. Fortunately, he slipped out unnoticed, and no one called the police.

Are you trying to make yourself comfortable in the

wrong "house"? Are you wondering what your strengths and purpose might be, what your gifts are? Discovering who we are as children of God can be an ongoing journey. Many of us can get bogged down in wondering how we stack up to others or questioning what we might have to offer. Perhaps that's why Paul wrote to the Corinthians that those who compare themselves among themselves "are not wise" (2 Corinthians 10:12). When we look at ourselves as less than or feel that we don't have anything to offer, we have fallen into the trap of our enemy Satan, who would love to keep us from fulfilling the plans God has for us.

The only way to combat lies is with the truth of God's Word. The Bible tells us that we are each uniquely gifted and created by Him.

> God has given each of you a gift from his great variety of spiritual gifts. Use them well to serve one another. Do you have the gift of speaking? Then speak as though God himself were speaking through you. Do you have the gift of helping others? Do it with all the strength and energy that God supplies. Then everything you do will bring glory to God through Jesus Christ. All glory and power to him forever and ever! Amen. (1 Peter 4:10–11 NLT)

I once saw a bumper sticker that read, "My child is in the gifted program" at a particular school. I remember thinking, *Every child is gifted!* I could look at my own three children and see their strengths and individuality. They are gifted with intelligence and concern for others, but these gifts manifest themselves in different ways. My oldest son, J. T., has a brilliant, analytical mind. He far surpassed my intellectual capabilities so that by the time he was in the fifth grade and would share things with me, I would nod my head and "mm-hmm" a lot just to make him believe I knew what he was talking about! He also has an extremely sensitive and caring heart, which he sometimes tries to hide. It comes out as he quietly gives to others or sees needs that others seem to miss.

My second son, Ryan, has dyslexia. Where his brother breezed through school, Ryan struggled. I often told him that he had to work twice as hard as the rest of us just to read a single word. He had to know the way the letters should look, the way they looked to him, make the conversion in his mind, and put the word back together again just to read it! He was as smart as his brother, but it revealed itself in a different way. Where J. T. was methodical and analytical, Ryan was practical, hands on. He is a troubleshooter, a fixer. Where J. T. theorizes, Ryan digs in and figures it out. His heart is huge and generous. He's the guy that would give you the shirt he's wearing if you ripped yours and needed a new one.

My daughter, Emily, is also bright, and her intelligence is more of a mix of her brothers. She did very well academically, but she also has a good dose of common sense and can see the bigger picture. She has great compassion for others, but spiritually she sees mostly black and white, and that enables her to share hard truth in a loving way. Her wisdom sometimes astounds me. She's the first to offer her support and encouragement to family and friends, loyal to the core.

I love that my kids are so different from one another! While each one is gifted, and some of their gifts are the same, they look and act in ways distinct and separate from each other. As kids of the King, we are just like that—all gifted, diverse, and yet complementary to one another. Not only has God given each one of us spiritual gifts, He has given us personalities, talents, and passions that He desires us to use to further His kingdom. This seems to be a struggle for many on their road to discovering their identity in Christ. Somehow, it is easy enough to see others' gifts but so much harder to see our own. We say, "But I can't. . ." and fill in the blank of whatever abilities we see in the countless people around us to whom we compare ourselves. Comparing ourselves to others is not only foolish, it becomes an obstacle to discovering what it is that God has put inside us to use for Him. We often downplay or disregard what we esteem to be "not as good as" whoever we are looking at in comparison.

This was illustrated to me recently when I met Barb, who is a wonderfully gifted decorator. She began to ask God how He might use that to honor and glorify Him. She loved helping others turn their ordinary into extraordinary, to take what they already had and repurpose and reuse it to help make their home a haven. As she helped one overwhelmed working mom create a place that her family could gather and spend time together enjoying their surroundings and one another, she recognized that God had given her the ability to bless others. God placed within her a dream to continue to use her giftedness to help women and families create a place of beauty where love could grow and be nurtured.

As the idea was developed and became more defined, Barb found other women who said, "I want to help." These friends had thought they had no talents or gifts to offer—they only knew they enjoyed decorating or had painting or sewing or carpentry skills. The vision of working together sparked an explosion and Be a Blessing Design Team was born. For their first project they raised the funds to help a family with three terminally ill children. Their remodeling consisted of repairing a cracked foundation and remediating a mold problem in the basement, installing wheelchair ramps, and redecorating the children's bedrooms. What a gift for this family in need of encouragement, love, and support—all by women who thought they had nothing to offer!

What gifts and abilities do you have that are untapped and untouched because you haven't recognized what God can do when we simply offer back to Him what He has given us? That is exactly what Romans 12:3–5 is trying to tell us: God is the one responsible for the giving of the gift. Have you heard someone with a beautiful voice? God gave it to her. Know someone who can act or dance or has a way with the elderly? God instilled that in him. Romans 12:6–8 (NLT) goes on to say:

In his grace, God has given us different gifts for doing certain things well. So if God has given you

the ability to prophesy, speak out with as much
faith as God has given you. If your gift is serving
others, serve them well. If you are a teacher,
teach well. If your gift is to encourage others,
be encouraging. If it is giving, give generously.
If God has given you leadership ability, take the
responsibility seriously. And if you have a gift for
showing kindness to others, do it gladly.

This unique gifting comes from God to each one of us. *The Message* says that these various gifts originate in God's Spirit. It is His expression of power in us, that He is behind it, and that each of us is given something to do to show who God is to those around us. "Everyone gets in on it, everyone benefits. All kinds of things are handed out by the Spirit, and to all kinds of people! The variety is wonderful" (1 Corinthians 12:7 MSG). I love how it goes on to describe some of these spiritual gifts—clear understanding, simple trust—because it brings a fresh description of what these gifts might look like. We often overlook the gifts within us because they don't seem very special. But the point is, God is the One who makes those simple things powerful!

Solomon was the wisest man in the world (that always makes me laugh when I think about his not-so-wise choices in his seven hundred wives and three hundred concubines—just shows you we are not as smart as we think we are!). Still, he had some impressive wisdom to share:

Can You Tell This Is a Knockoff?

Enjoy what you have rather than desiring what you don't have. Just dreaming about nice things is meaningless—like chasing the wind. Everything has already been decided. It was known long ago what each person would be. So there's no use arguing with God about your destiny. (Ecclesiastes 6:9–10 NLT)

Psalm 139:13–16 in *The Message* describes this beautifully:

Oh yes, you shaped me first inside, then out; you formed me in my mother's womb. I thank you, High God—you're breathtaking! Body and soul, I am marvelously made! I worship in adoration—what a creation! You know me inside and out, you know every bone in my body; you know exactly how I was made, bit by bit, how I was sculpted from nothing into something. Like an open book, you watched me grow from conception to birth; all the stages of my life were spread out before you, the days of my life all prepared before I'd even lived one day.

God created you to be uniquely *you*! No one else can do your job, fulfill your purpose, or impact those in your sphere of influence in the way God made you to interact and be a blessing to others. Do you believe that? If we did, we would have less of a struggle with knowing who we are in Christ.

As women, we can be pretty good at masking our true feelings. We like looking good on the outside, no matter what is going on inside. See if you can relate to this story someone sent to me recently in an e-mail:

Jennifer's wedding day was fast approaching. Nothing could dampen her excitement—not even her parents' nasty divorce. She wanted everything perfect, including the mother-of-the-bride dress, which was second only to her own as the bride. Jennifer had gone shopping with her mother, and they had found the perfect dress for her mom. A short time later, Jennifer was horrified to learn that her father's new young wife had bought the exact same dress! Jennifer asked her to exchange it, but she refused. "Absolutely not, I look like a million bucks in this dress, and I'm wearing it," her stepmother replied. Upset and crying, Jennifer told her mother, who graciously said, "Never mind, sweetheart. I'll get another dress. After all, it's your special day." A few days later, they went shopping and found another gorgeous dress. When they stopped for lunch, Jennifer asked her mother, "Aren't you going to return the other dress? You really don't have another occasion where you could wear it." Her mother just smiled and replied, "Of course I do, dear. I'm wearing it to the rehearsal dinner the night before the wedding."

I laughed when I read this story, too, mostly because

Can You Tell This Is a Knockoff?

I could see myself so clearly in the bride's mother. As I struggled to discover my own true identity in Christ I became very good at disguising myself. I hid behind a mask of what I thought others expected me to look like. No matter that it wasn't really who I was. I wanted to be what I thought I *should* be. It took another story for the Lord to begin unveiling the real me and to help me see that pretending to be someone else was really an artificial faith. A knockoff of what God had created me to be.

When my youngest child was about five years old I went away on a weekend retreat with an old friend from college. One of the ladies who spoke at that conference shared a story she heard at the dinner table of a pastor. He had been in an airport waiting on a flight when he heard a great commotion. A crowd gathered and seemed to be following two ladies down the concourse. Like everyone else, he was curious and turned to see what was going on. There was a woman walking with a stewardess—the two of them were laughing and talking and somehow managing to ignore the staring and pointing people. No, it wasn't a celebrity. The woman walking with the stewardess had a growth that stretched from her shoulder nearly to the top of her head. Even with all the information available about disabilities on television and the Internet, I know that didn't prevent people from gawking.

The pastor was intrigued by this young woman who, despite the disfigurement and negative attention, radiated joy and contentment. When she sat in a waiting-room chair near him, the pastor slipped into the seat beside her.

"Excuse me," he said gently, "I don't mean to pry, but you are so obviously joyful and seem so undisturbed by all the stares and comments—I just have to ask you how you are able to do it."

This precious young woman explained that she was born with this deformity, and the tentacles of the growth were so entangled in her brain that trying to remove it would bring certain death. So, in order to live, she had to live with the deformity. Surgery wasn't an option. She shared with the pastor that her mother, in shame and embarrassment, rejected her, and this young girl had led a very lonely life until she reached her teens and met a youth pastor who shared with her how much Christ loved her and how He died for her. This man's acceptance and love and the church's embrace helped her grow and mature in her faith. Now, as a young woman, she spent her time going into hospitals and talking with burn victims and other patients with deformities to help them cope and give them hope in Christ.

I was transfixed by this story. I just kept thinking— that's me. That woman is *me*. Oh, my deformities weren't visible. I wore my disfigurement, my misshapenness, on the inside. But if anyone could see it they would reject me and murmur and point and exclaim out loud—"Look at that ugly woman!" I struggled with the fear that if people truly knew who I was they would not want anything to do with me. I lived with the lie that God couldn't love me, couldn't use me, that I was deficient and unworthy. I ignored the truth of God's Word that calls me His child, that tells me my true identity, the core of who I am, is

Can You Tell This Is a Knockoff?

hidden in Christ, and it is He who makes me worthy. I am forever grateful to this unknown young woman who lived her life in such authentic faith so confident of who she was in Christ that she could be used for God to reach countless untold people and change lives—namely, mine.

We often look for greatness to use for God, but God looks for someone He can use to display *His* greatness. Paul wrote in 1 Corinthians 1:27 (NIV), "But God chose the foolish things of the world to shame the wise; God chose the weak things of the world to shame the strong." God doesn't *need* us! He gives us opportunity to be His vessels—to allow His love and grace, mercy and power to flow through us so that *He* can touch the hearts and lives of people around us. We get to be part of His grand scheme, His larger purpose. Like a mother who lets her small child "help" her clean or bake, I'm sure there are more times when we get in His way rather than actually help, but God in His graciousness allows us to use what gifts we have.

Whatever your gifts might be, their purpose is to edify the body (Ephesians 4:11–12). The Greek word found in this passage is *oikodome* and has the idea of "building up," promoting growth, wisdom, and holiness in others. The gifts God gives us are never for ourselves; they are always for others' edification—to build them up and help them grow. The flipside is that when we use our gifts for others, we grow as well. That's just how God does things!

Paul tells us in 1 Corinthians 15 that he is who he is by God's grace, and that grace should not be wasted, or as the New King James Version puts it in verse ten, "His grace toward me was not in vain." Although Paul at this point was an apostle and a devoted follower of Christ, he describes how he once fervently persecuted believers. Only God can make that kind of transformation in a life and turn it around to do His work in His way. The thing to remember is that Paul was already gifted before he began the work of an apostle. God created him, gifted him, for His own purposes. All that passion that was so evident in Paul's learning and studying and zeal for what was "right"—though it was misguided—was the gifting God had already placed within Paul so that he could fulfill the plans God had for him.

Timothy was Paul's young protégé. He had been raised by a godly mother and grandmother and followed Paul into a life of ministry. He was Paul's "son in the faith" (1 Timothy 1:2 NKJV). Paul's letters to him were words of encouragement as he endeavored to help Timothy as a young leader of the early church. He advises him to not let anyone disparage him because of his youth, to stand firm against false teaching, and to fight "the good fight" (2 Timothy 4:7) for the faith. In 2 Timothy Paul expresses his thankfulness for Timothy and for his spiritual heritage; he admonishes him to not be ashamed of the Lord and to "hold fast" to Paul's sound words of doctrine and teaching. He also encourages Timothy to be "strong in the grace that is in Christ Jesus" (2 Timothy 2:1 NKJV) and to "stir up the gift of God" (2 Timothy 1:6 NKJV) or as the New International Version puts it, "I remind you to fan into flame the gift of God, which is in you."

You have this same God-given grace and gifting.

It looks different for each one of us—and that's the beauty of it! We are all unique, made for a purpose—His purpose. Our identities are found in Him, not in ourselves. This is the opposite of what the world tells us—"be all you can be," "I did it my way," "Because you're worth it"—but the world is an enemy of God (James 4:4), and we must caution ourselves so we aren't swayed by its philosophies. God is the giver of all good gifts (James 1:17), and Paul tells us in Romans 7:18 (NIV), "For I know that good itself does not dwell in me, that is, in my sinful nature." It is God within us that is good. He gifts us and empowers that gifting.

God used a simple Jewish girl to carry the Savior of the world, a shepherd boy to defeat a giant and become a great king, a band of unschooled fishermen and rabbi-rejects to change the world. When you look at the heroes in the "hall of fame" in Hebrews 11, what you see is not a litany of amazing individuals but one of ordinary people that God used in extraordinary ways. The common denominator that allowed them to be vessels for God's greatness was their faith— not in themselves but *in God* and His ability and power. Their gifts came from God, and it was their dependence on Him that made them exceptional and helped them accomplish amazing feats of faith. Verse six of that chapter tells us that it is impossible for any of us to please God without that same kind of faith—faith *in Him* not in our own abilities (which we did not provide for ourselves).

This faith gave them spiritual eyes to see beyond the world they were physically living in (v. 13). With this perspective, they looked past their own capabilities and trusted God to do the work in and through them. They recognized that their gifts and abilities came from God and were His to use as He wanted to use them. They trusted God to fulfill His plans. We have that same opportunity.

Do you see yourself in Moses, who thought he wasn't eloquent of speech but whom God called to go head-to-head with Pharoah? Or Rahab, whose past was one that might have haunted her, yet God used her to carry on the righteous earthly line of Christ our Savior? Are you in the same situation as Joseph, betrayed and wrongfully accused and rejected by family? God used him to save a nation! Maybe you see yourself as a Sarah or Hannah or Elizabeth whose barrenness marked the disappointment of life not turning out as they expected. God used each of them to raise sons who were faithful men of God.

What do we have to offer our Creator except what He has already given us? Hebrews 12 tells us that we have these great examples of faith listed in chapter eleven so that we can find the strength and endurance for our own race—to use our own gifts that God has bestowed on us and to make sure that no one "gets left out of God's generosity" (Hebrews 12:15 MSG). The New International Version and the New King James Version both say that we should make sure no one "fall[s] short of the grace of God"; the New Living Translation puts it this way: "Look after each other so that none of you fails to receive the grace of God."

God's grace, which was bestowed while we were

sinners (Romans 5:8), is undeserved and more than we can obtain for ourselves. It is the same grace we live in day by day and the same grace we need so that we can be available to God, so that our gifts can be used to honor and glorify Him and to edify the Body of Christ. Our gifts are given *by* Him to use *for* Him. To not use those gifts that He gives us is an affront and offense. It is in essence rejecting what He's given us. His grace, His mercy, His love, His forgiveness, His redemption—He has given us all we need to fulfill the purpose He has for us.

> *I always thank my God for you because of his grace given you in Christ Jesus. For in him you have been enriched in every way—with all kinds of speech and with all knowledge—God thus confirming our testimony about Christ among you. Therefore you do not lack any spiritual gift as you eagerly wait for our Lord Jesus Christ to be revealed. He will also keep you firm to the end, so that you will be blameless on the day of our Lord Jesus Christ. God is faithful, who has called you into fellowship with his Son, Jesus Christ our Lord.* (1 Corinthians 1:4–9 NIV)

Discussion Questions

1. List some things you are good at or are passionate about. Do you see these as God-given? ....
   ....
   ....

2. Have you compared yourself with others? How did this make you feel? Read 2 Corinthians 10:12 in The Message. What was Paul's conclusion about comparisons? ....
   ....
   ....

3. Make a short list of some of the people you know and the gifts you see in their lives. According to 1 Corinthians 12:4 who distributes the spiritual gifts in our lives? ....
   ....
   ....

4. Read James 1:17. Where does every good and perfect gift come from? ....
   ....
   ....

5. Romans 11:11–24 describes how the Gentiles were grafted in and now share in the same inheritance as the Jews. Read Romans 11:29. What does it say about God's gifts and His call? ....

....

....

6. Read Judges 4:1–23. Who did God use to defeat Israel's enemies when Barak hesitated in trusting the Lord? What lesson can we learn from this piece of Israel's history? ....

....

....

7. Write out Matthew 7:11. Ask God to reveal the gifts He has already given you. ....

....

....

Notes:

CHAPTER FOUR
Free to Forgive

All this comes from the God who settled the relationship between us and him, and then called us to settle our relationships with each other. . . . God has given us the task of telling everyone what he is doing. We're Christ's representatives. God uses us to persuade men and women to drop their differences and enter into God's work of making things right between them. We're speaking for Christ himself now: Become friends with God; he's already a friend with you. How? you ask. In Christ. God put the wrong on him who never did anything wrong, so we could be put right with God.

2 CORINTHIANS 5:18–21 MSG

$\mathcal{I}$ listened to the conversation of a couple that had been married for seventy-two years. Each spouse was ninety-six years old. I love these people dearly, and not meaning any disrespect, listening to their conversation was comical to say the least. She began, "I turned up the heat so you wouldn't be cold." He looked at her, cupped his ear to hear her better, and shouted, "WHAT?" With a look of irritation, she repeated louder, "I TURNED UP THE HEAT SO YOU WOULDN'T BE COLD!" Pausing, he looked at her with his eyebrows furrowed slightly then shouted back, "I KNOW THIS IS A NICE SHIRT. I LIKE IT SO MUCH!"

With a sigh here, a roll of the eyes there, and even a wave of the hand in exasperation, the conversation continued and developed into a minor and amusing conflict. But unfortunately, most conflict in our relationships doesn't border on amusing and even more so, doesn't stay minor. Whether it is planning for the holidays with family, an argument with our spouse, a friend who said something hurtful, or debating whose turn it is to take out the trash—no matter how hard we try to deny it or run from it, conflict finds us one way or another.

I remember the day I walked out of church as a Christian. That morning, I had stepped forward and received the forgiveness that Jesus offered me. Twenty-three years old and pregnant with our first son, I had surrendered and given my heart and life to Christ. I looked at my husband and exclaimed in awe, "I feel so free!" The colors of creation shown that much brighter, and I literally felt that much lighter (remember, I was seven months pregnant, and when you're that far along you don't feel light, so you know it was supernatural).

My sin, which had caused a gaping chasm between God and I, had been wiped away. The wrath that I deserved, Jesus had received. The hostility between God and I came to an end, and peace took its place. This peace was nothing I deserved or made happen. God alone initiated reconciliation with me, and because of Jesus paying the price, He forgave me and restored our relationship. He names you and I "forgiven" and His peace and favor rest on us (Luke 2:14).

God's forgiveness is hard to understand and wrap our minds around, because we all have thought at one time or another, *I've done too many stupid and horrible things, I don't deserve to be forgiven, I'm not worthy, I can't be forgiven.* We're right in part. We don't deserve it, we're not worthy, and we've made many bad decisions. But the truth is we *are* forgiven in Jesus. We can't earn this forgiveness; it can only be *received* as a gift. God looks at us, smiles at us, loves us, and reaches out to us holding the gift.

We all have fallen short of the glory of God (Romans 3:23). We all have sinned and "missed the mark" countless times. There is no way we can reach the standards of a holy and perfect God. That's why this gift of forgiveness is so incredibly priceless and is worthy to be celebrated! What we need, He has, and He longs to give it to us. What makes this reconciliation so out of the ordinary is that God chooses to reconcile with us even when we are His enemies (Romans 5:9–11). He bought us back from the clutches of our Enemy with His very life. He has wiped out our sin, past, present, and future—removed every single one as far as the east is from the west (Psalm 103:12) and made us whiter than snow (Psalm 51:7). His perfection covers our imperfection. We don't have to live in failure or defeat. With His forgiveness, we are set free from the prison that once held us in darkness, free from guilt and shame, free from condemnation, free from hell and eternal separation from God, free from fear and living this life alone. Not only has He rescued us, He also has taken up residence within us and wants to live through us (1 Corinthians 6:17; Galatians 2:20). He has given us a new identity and a ministry as well—a ministry of reconciliation (2 Corinthians 5:18–21).

As His ambassadors and representatives, we have a message of reconciliation to spread. Because when you've been sitting in the dank, dark prison cell for years on end, you can't help but shout about the One who unlocked the door. There are multitudes of people who are still sitting behind bars, waiting to hear the news that God wants them, that their guilt has been wiped away, and that they can have abundant life in Jesus. Many of those people are right under our noses—people we work beside, rub shoulders with on committees, spend time with at the coffee shop, and even worship with at our church. Obviously we can share with others who God is and what

He has done in our lives through our words, but what sticks with others is what we live out. We show others God's character by allowing Him to live through ours.

God is growing us to look more like Him, and because of that He gives us all kinds of opportunities to live out reconciliation. Wherever we live and work with people, there is going to be conflict. You know exactly what I'm talking about. And if you're like most people, you hate dealing with conflict. Conflicts are challenging, draining, and difficult. They can be uncomfortable when they reveal to us some of our own weaknesses and shortcomings. But because of our identity of "forgiven" and the security and rest we have in Jesus, He walks with us every step of the way as we sort it out. As we work with Him and let Him lead us through it, He reveals Himself in powerful and healing ways.

Several years ago, I had gone through a painful time of conflict. It was awful. It was full of injustice, times of pulling the plank out of my own eye and looking at my own unhealthy tendencies (Matthew 7:1–5). It was marked with tears, heartache, confusion, frustration, and anger. But the lesson I learned was that God works in us and teaches through conflict. He doesn't give up on us or distance Himself from us but instead comes near and shines through the pain. My husband commented several times throughout the ordeal that he saw God in the way I was responding. I don't say that to boast in my efforts, because I felt like a complete mess. I say that to boast in the Lord because it was His power and Spirit that was visible. It was His strength that carried me through the storm and His unfailing grace that taught me more about who He is and who I am in Him as a minister of reconciliation.

My boys are currently eating us out of house and home. They are fifteen, thirteen, and eleven—very wonderful, active, and growing young men. The store has become my second home, my new best friend is the checkout lady, and the delivery truck driver stocking the bread aisle knows my name. However, there are times that the boys will get up in the morning, open the cupboard, and be struck with the fact that their favorite cereal is gone and options are limited. As they express their displeasure, my nurturing response is something like, "Sorry, I don't have it. If I had it, it'd be yours. But I can't give you what I don't have." So, until I can hop in my van and head "home" to spend time with family and friends, they will go without. Whether it is food from the pantry, cash for a candy bar, or a coveted video game, if I don't have it, I can't give it.

And so it is with forgiveness. Only when we receive God's forgiveness can we forgive others from the heart. We can't give what we don't have. Let's look at our relationships—our spouses, children, people at church that fray our nerves, the picky neighbor across the street, the coworker we try to avoid, or all those difficult people in our lives. How are we handling those relationships when it comes to conflict? If forgiveness and reconciliation are God's heartbeat, why would it be any different when it comes to our relationships with others? We may do well at telling others about God's heart of love and forgiveness, but we may feel justified in hardening our own hearts in unforgiveness when somebody makes us angry.

God says (through Paul), "If it is possible, as far as it depends on you, live at peace with everyone" (Romans 12:18 NIV) and "Let us therefore make every effort to do what leads to peace and to mutual edification" (Romans 14:19 NIV). In other words, we should do all we can to lift one another up. When conflict comes knocking, rather than looking at our own hearts and responsibility in resolving it, we usually spend most of the time judging the hearts and responsibilities of those who have hurt us. Rather than lifting up with our words, we tend to tear down. Rather than attempting to understand by listening to another's perspective, we defend ours. As believers, God lives in us. He reminds us of the seriousness of hurting one another with our anger and the priority of reconciling (Matthew 5:21–24). He instructs us to avoid sinning in our anger (Ephesians 4:26), warns us of the danger of being easily angered (Ecclesiastes 7:9) and the consequences of unforgiveness (Matthew 6:14–15).

So, when it comes to conflict, what knockoff mentality do we carry? I believe it is forgetfulness or "spiritual amnesia," and it is rooted in pride and fear. We forget the gravity of our sin and what it cost our Savior to pay for it. When we're offended, thoughts like these spring into action: *I have rights so I must defend myself. . . . I have to win, so I will attack you, talk to others to gain support, or see things only how I believe them to be. I will do whatever it takes to prove I'm right. . . . I hate conflict and*

don't want to deal with this. I would rather walk away from
this relationship than do what I can to bring healing. . . .
You're asking for forgiveness? I'll think about it. . . ."

It is our natural tendency to preserve and uphold
our rights over doing what it takes to reconcile. And as
we hold on to our hurts and withhold forgiveness, we
willingly place the chains around our ankles, attach the
lock, and click it shut. I've heard it said, "Unforgiveness
is like drinking poison and waiting for someone else to
die." As much as we want the person that hurt us to feel
their "wrong," when we choose to harbor grudges, the
unforgiveness, hurt, and anger eat us alive. We're the
ones who suffer. But with Jesus, there's a different option.
Because Jesus has given us forgiveness, we can give it
to the next person. The spiritual "cupboards" aren't bare.
Jesus has filled them, and there is an endless supply to
give away.

When it comes to conflict, God has shown me there
is a bigger picture involved. April 19, 1995, is a day
few of us will ever forget. The Alfred P. Murrah federal
building in Oklahoma City, which housed government
offices and a day-care center, was destroyed in a deadly
terrorist attack. The explosion killed one hundred sixty-
eight people, nineteen of them children, and injured more
than eight hundred others. Several years ago while on
vacation, our family stopped to visit the National Memorial
and Museum in Oklahoma City on the site of where this
tragedy took place. When we stepped onto the grounds
it was powerfully quiet, almost as if we could feel that
something significant happened there. In front of the

museum was a wall made of tiles that had been collected from children in Oklahoma City and other cities across our nation and Canada. Each tile was the tablet for a picture or a sentiment of comfort and hope from the heart of a child—pictures of our nation's flag, the peace symbol, hearts, rainbows, crosses, and statements like, "God is with you."

But there was one tile I will never forget. A bright yellow sun and a big red heart bordered this tile, but in the center, written in simple handwriting, was the age-old question we've been trying to wrap our minds around for years: "Can't we all just get along?" The tragedy that occurred in Oklahoma City didn't just affect those one thousand individuals that were killed or injured. The evil that was done didn't only affect their friends and families, or even just their city. This attack affected our nation and our world, from the oldest to the youngest.

"Can't we all just get along?" As adults, this question may stir in us complicated responses and explanations of why we can't get along with certain people, or why we choose to hold on to our hurts and anger, but from the heart of a child this question seems pretty simple—and wise. I had a difficult relationship that had been characterized by conflict for many years. As I sat across the table from my mentor talking about this relationship, she encouraged me with these wise words: "Use healthy and God-honoring boundaries so you can go the distance—but whatever you do, if at all possible, do not cut this person off."

I have to admit, I was a little disappointed. I was at a

point in life where I was emotionally exhausted and had nothing else to give to this relationship. But I chose to listen and God has done the miraculous. Even though this relationship has its difficulties, He has brought forgiveness and healing by teaching and transforming my heart and mind. He has changed my perspective.

I've known from reading God's Word that God's heartbeat is unity in the Body of Christ (Psalm 133:1; Ephesians 4:3; Galatians 5:13–15). We may be wired with varied personalities, tastes, or spiritual gifts, and that's a beautiful thing. God has made us each different to complement one another so the team functions at its best (1 Corinthians 12:12–31). But unity means that even in our diversity, we are guided by the Holy Spirit, functioning as one, serving one another, headed the same direction, as we work together toward the same goal (Philippians 2:2–4). God wants to grow us up spiritually, emotionally, and mentally as individuals *and* grow us together as the Body of Christ—serving Jesus and looking like Him more and more (Ephesians 4:13–16). Our unity reveals to the world that God loves us just as much as He loves Jesus (John 17:23). Basically, our unity is a witnessing tool that shines Jesus to the world.

I've also known that God's heart and character are those of forgiveness and reconciliation (Exodus 34:6–7; Psalm 86:5; Matthew 18:21–35; Luke 23:34; 1 John 1:9). God has been teaching me more of His heart and the pain of broken relationships in His body. I have listened to people speak of the same past hurts repeatedly, continuing to sit in their chains. Instead of forgiving and looking forward, they continue to focus on their woundedness. They are miserable and drain others of energy whenever they're around. I have also experienced personally the hurt and confusion of a severed relationship. Remembering my mentor's wise counsel, I have realized that the detonated "bomb" of unresolved conflict, hurt, and anger between you and I doesn't just affect us. Its impact is spread wide and can penetrate deep, throwing debris and wounding those inside and outside the Body of Christ.

Some of the far-reaching and damaging debris I have seen in many women concerns issues of trust. We've been hurt profoundly by people in our past. We've grown up in homes where significant people in our lives "dropped the ball" and our trust as little ones was shattered. We've been betrayed by spouses, friends, parents, children, you name it. Many of us have suffered abuse at the hands of someone who was supposed to have our best interest at heart and didn't. We live in a broken world with broken people. It doesn't make it right, but we know hurting people hurt other people. So, it makes sense why mistrust might reign in our hearts and relationships.

Wounds from our past and the lessons we've learned from them can bring wisdom to our present relationships. There may be people in our lives who display a pattern of behavior. For example, maybe you have a friend who can't keep a secret. That doesn't mean you stop loving her or you aren't nice to her. That doesn't mean you have nothing to do with her. It just means you don't tell her what you don't want shared with others. Being cautious with our trust can be wise. That being said, I wonder how big a part unforgiveness plays in preventing us from trusting. Let me explain.

Tanya had every reason not to trust anyone. In her eyes, people weren't trustworthy and vulnerability only led to getting hurt. This young woman had been sexually, verbally, and physically abused from the age of two into her teen years. Her abusers ranged from family members to complete strangers coming in and out of her mother's life. As a little girl, she not only took the role of caregiver to her addict mother, but she also endured torture and even physical imprisonment in a bathroom day after day. Tanya's mother was all she had, until the day her mother dropped her off with Tanya's grandfather and his wife. Not only did her mother abandon her, but she also gave Tanya to the very person who had sexually abused her when she was a little girl. For five years Tanya endured his abuse until despite his threats, she finally disclosed what had been occurring.

The end of her abuse had come, but the physical and emotional repercussions would continue. Hospitalization for severe depression, cutting, bulimia, attempted suicide, intense loneliness, and mistrust were all wrapped in the insatiable longing to be loved. Hate for her mother filled Tanya's heart for not protecting her, for not being the mother Tanya needed her to be. Wanting a new beginning, Tanya married a wonderful man but soon discovered their relationship was missing foundational essentials—trust, healthy communication, and emotional and physical intimacy. Her relationships with other women also were impacted, as Tanya looked to them to fill a void her mother had left.

Years later she entered counseling and worked through her pain, grieved the loss of a mother she never had as well as the news of her death. She forgave her mother for who she was and what she never became—the mother Tanya needed her to be. Facing her trust issues enabled Tanya to become aware of her tendency to guard herself, but forgiveness gave her the courage to step out and go forward. Forgiveness let her begin to take baby steps in becoming vulnerable, with her husband and in her friendships. Her life has never been the same—her marriage is growing into the healthy one she dreamed of, and her relationships with other women are marked with encouraging transparency. Today she shares her story, the power of forgiveness, the truth of the Gospel, and her faith in Jesus with women everywhere (see *www.myfathersdaughter.com*).

Tanya's story is an intense one, and while we may not know that kind of experience, many of us have been hurt by others. One woman shared with me about her father's infidelity and how it has impacted her relationship with her husband. When it came to her husband's interaction with other women, she became hyper-vigilant to the point of bringing strife into their marriage. She went on to say that forgiving her father was the key to killing her mistrust. The most important man in her life as a child had chosen the wrong path. But the most important man in her life as a woman, her husband, hasn't. She could rest in the fact that her husband isn't her father, and to "try" him as guilty was unjust and damaging. When she would feel uneasy, she would recognize where her feelings stemmed from but respond in a much healthier way. Forgiveness won, and their marriage grew stronger.

Many of us may become angry when someone unknowingly touches on a wound inflicted years ago that we never dealt with. We may not see that. We're just angry. So we hold grudges against others because of our perceived hurt. We need to stop and ask if we have examined the layers of our trust issues. Are our relationships today affected by wounds from our past that we haven't let go of and given to God?

So, how do we forgive those who have hurt us? We process our anger and hurt with a trusted friend or even a counselor, but ultimately we have to take it to God—our situation, our feelings, the people involved, the whole mess of it. With God, we can "tell on" others and what they did to us. We can tell Him how it made us feel, how angry, hurt, or confused we are. We can be blatantly honest about it all. Just read through the Psalms. David wasn't shy about putting it out there with God. A dear friend of mine who is also a respected counselor says an important first step toward forgiveness and healing is not burying our hurt but looking at and processing it so we can move forward.

We can tell God about our hurt, but moving forward is giving it up. We can give our situation, our feelings, and our offender all over to God. One of the beautiful things about God is that He's big enough to handle our stuff.

His lap is big enough to hold our conflict, our feelings, and our offender. We can give it all to Him and choose to leave it there. We can walk away with His promise that He will provide all that we need—forgiveness, love, strength, courage, desire, and even eyes to see the bigger picture. Then we choose. Forgiveness is not a feeling. Forgiveness is a choice we make as we rest in our relationship with Jesus.

Years ago, a friend and I had a disagreement, and as I processed my feelings and looked at the situation, I knew I needed to apologize. I did so but never received one in return. Pride began to wave its hand, "Pick me, pick me!" Unfortunately I did, so as days and weeks went on, I found myself struggling with anger and the fact that she didn't apologize to me. Finally, sick of being miserable and not wanting to stay a prisoner of anger and unforgiveness, I realized I couldn't take responsibility for her choice. I knew God was asking me to deal with my heart, not hers. Because I've been given the identity of "forgiven" and the message of Jesus' forgiveness, I chose to forgive. When I woke up in the morning and feelings of anger came to my heart and mind, I took them to God, and He provided me the grace and strength to rest in forgiveness again that day. God alone, moment by moment and day after day, worked in my heart and renewed my thoughts. His peace and forgiveness replaced my anger.

One thing I have learned regarding conflict is that there are two sides to every story, and therefore two hearts that are wounded. Just because I want to be

Can You Tell This Is a Knockoff?

"right" in the conflict doesn't mean I am. As I hand over my hurts to Him, in order to take ownership in the conflict I also need to ask Him to show me my sin and my skewed perspective and confess it to Him (Psalm 139:23–24; Psalm 51). Sometimes I can be easily offended or may see things only from a biased perspective because of an old wound. I may believe things that aren't really so. There have been many times that God has shown me my sin — my bad attitude, my overreaction, my hurtful words — and I have had to return in humility to extend a sincere apology for the hurt I delivered.

In the early years of our marriage my conflict resolution skills weren't the healthiest. I reacted the same way every time, and in the process, I didn't hear Bruce's heart in the heat of our conflict. It wasn't until something divisive attempted to wedge its way into our marriage that my eyes and ears were opened. I began to pray that God would take my walls of defense down so I could hear the message underneath the emotion. It is important to be aware of how we respond in conflict — defensiveness, yelling, leaving the scene, gossiping, blaming, making excuses, shutting down and not communicating — and learn what changes we need to make so we don't continue getting the same result. Too many times, the change is simply listening.

When we genuinely forgive from the heart (Matthew 18:35), we can let the offense go, and the chains that once bound us fall to the ground. The offense stops boiling over in our speech through gossip and is no longer present as the poison of malice or revenge in our emotions and thoughts. It doesn't emanate from the deepest part of our being. That doesn't mean we don't remember it and learn from it. That doesn't mean we don't use the lessons we learned to teach others. That doesn't mean we don't see the damage the hurt has caused and understand how it has affected us, but we don't hold the unrest in our hearts anymore or use it as ammunition. We can go forward and take responsibility with what we will do with it. Instead of pain, our hearts can hold peace.

We can pray blessing upon that person (Luke 6:27–31; Romans 12:14), praying God would give him or her all that is needed and shower blessings however He desires. That is God working in and through us. When we take it to God and let Him do the work in our hearts, we can forgive those who hurt us whether they ask us for forgiveness or not. If they apologize and ask for forgiveness, it is a sweet time to be able to verbalize it and experience reconciliation. With our new identity rooted in Jesus, forgiveness and reconciliation can be a reality. We have received His forgiveness, and as His ambassadors, we carry that message to all we encounter (Colossians 3:12–13; Matthew 18:21–35).

Some of you may say, "But you don't know what she has done to me. Jesus is asking the impossible" or "You don't understand how badly he has hurt me. I don't know if I can forgive him." You aren't alone. Jesus' disciples struggled with the same thing. In Luke 17, Jesus talks about offenses. He tells the disciples that when others sin against them they are to correct their offender. The heart of Jesus comes out in this command, as this word "rebuke" means to correct but to do so tentatively and allow for explanation. They were to speak truth but graciously; they were to genuinely listen and attempt to understand another's viewpoint. Jesus concludes by telling them to forgive repeatedly when they are sinned against.

With these overwhelming and seemingly impossible commands, His disciples look at Him and exclaim, "Increase our faith!" And the faith He gives is exactly what it takes to forgive from the heart—faith in Him, His power, His security, His love, and His forgiveness so we can let go and surrender our rights, fear, and pride. With Jesus, forgiveness from the heart is possible, because it comes through Him. With Jesus, we can be women of grace, forgiveness, and peace. That doesn't mean we're doormats, aren't firm when needed, or don't speak truth in love. But our end goal is always forgiveness and reconciliation. (It should be stated here that for those of us who have experienced abuse, reconciliation isn't always possible without life change. But forgiveness is. Those of us who must relate to toxic people, God-honoring boundaries are essential while keeping our hearts steeped in forgiveness.)

"If it is possible, as far as it depends on you, live at peace with everyone" (Romans 12:18 NIV). With forgiveness and reconciliation as our goal, what if we sincerely apologize and the person doesn't forgive us or want to reconcile? Then it is out of our control. We may need to grieve the loss of that friendship, but we can have peace knowing we were obedient to our Father's heart.

Oftentimes one of the hardest people to forgive is the one we look at in the mirror every day. A woman once told me she had an abortion more than thirty years earlier, and she cannot forgive herself. She continues to carry her guilt. Jesus' words to her and to all who carry the burden of guilt are: *"It's time to lay it down."* "The kingdom of God has come near. Repent and *believe* the good news!" (Mark 1:15 NIV). Jesus invites us, "Come to me, all you who are weary and burdened, and I will give you rest. Take my yoke upon you and learn from me, for I am gentle and humble in heart, and you will find rest for your souls. For my yoke is easy and my burden is light" (Matthew 11:28–30 NIV).

Go to Jesus. No matter what we've done, we have a "Come to me" kind of God. John tells us in 1 John 1:9 (NIV), "If we confess our sins, he is faithful and just and will forgive us our sins and purify us from all unrighteousness." God forgave us thousands of years ago for what we did yesterday, for the hurtful thing we'll say tomorrow, and for the poor choice we'll make next year. I'm not condoning a "let's sin, because He'll forgive us anyway" kind of mentality. I'm saying let's receive and live in forgiveness, in the gift He's given, in the identity He's named us, in all that He has for us, and in all that He is. Like we walk and breathe in air, we walk and breathe in forgiveness.

When we sin, let's talk to Him about it. Confession to Jesus means admitting our wrong and agreeing with Him that we messed up, that we sinned, that we fell short. As we agree with Him in our genuine sorrow, we have the privilege of *experiencing* His forgiveness and cleansing that He has already provided! There is nothing more we can add to the punishment—our guilt, our shame, the condemnation we carry on our backs won't contribute to the payment for our sins. Jesus has experienced all that for us on the cross, and the price of our sin has been paid in full. He has given us His righteousness (2 Corinthians 5:21) and declares, "It is finished" (John 19:30 NIV). The choice is ours to believe it and receive it. We have been set free to forgive! And in forgiving, we carry His message and show Him to the world.

Discussion Questions

1. Everybody experiences conflict. How do you tend to deal with conflict in your relationships? ....
   ....
   ....

2. Share a time when you experienced conflict. What did you learn? How did God reveal Himself? ....
   ....
   ....

3. How have you seen unresolved conflict in your life affect others? ....
   ....
   ....

4. Read 2 Corinthians 5:18–20 (NIV). What does it mean to you to have a ministry of reconciliation? To be called an ambassador of Christ (what is an ambassador's job)? ....
   ....
   ....

5. We can't give what we don't have. Have you received God's forgiveness? Is there guilt or condemnation that

Can You Tell This Is a Knockoff?

you carry that you haven't taken to Jesus and laid down? If you have, have you left it there and forgiven yourself? ....

....

....

6. Would you describe yourself as someone with trust issues? If so, have you ever talked with someone (a friend or Christian counselor) about them in order to move forward? Has unforgiveness had any part in hindering your trust level with others? ....

....

....

7. Do you hold unforgiveness in your heart toward another or need to be reconciled with anyone? How can you live out Romans 12:18, "As far as it depends on you. . ." and take the first steps toward healing and forgiveness? ....

....

....

Will you make today the day you choose forgiveness? Whether forgiving yourself or someone else, will you allow Jesus to unlock your prison door and walk forward with Him hand in hand? Share with someone else your decision and enjoy freedom! ....

....

....

Notes:

....
....
....
....
....
....
....
....
....
....
....
....
....
....
....
....
....
....
....
....
....
....
....
....
....

CHAPTER FIVE
Powered by Purpose

We have different gifts, according to the grace given to each of us. If your gift is prophesying, then prophesy in accordance with your faith; if it is serving, then serve; if it is teaching, then teach; if it is to encourage, then give encouragement; if it is giving, then give generously; if it is to lead, do it diligently; if it is to show mercy, do it cheerfully.

ROMANS 12:6–9 NIV

$\mathcal{I}$ pulled into the outside drive-through lane at the local bank, but I didn't get close enough to reach the canister in the air tube. So I slipped off my seat belt and leaned out the open window but still couldn't reach it! I grabbed the door handle to open the car door, but the only problem was our car was a late model Nissan—one with an automatic seat belt. So when I opened the door with my head still out of the window, the seat belt slid down and trapped my head in the corner of the window. Did I mention I worked at this bank? And that it was my day off and all of my coworkers were at the window having a great laugh at my expense?

Sometimes we get trapped in living our lives without full use of the power available to us. Maybe we've recognized the talents and gifts that God has given us. Perhaps we've heard Him speak into our lives about how and where He wants us to use these gifts. We may have received a "calling," a nudging in our spirits or a longing and desire to do a specific task for God. But it doesn't work out as we've planned. It's not as easy as it should be. We're struggling with putting it all together.

When my daughter Emily got married, she planned and organized everything. From the flowers (blue hydrangeas, white roses, and butterfly nights) to the venue (a country club at a local golf course with a gorgeous pond and gazebo) to the white horse-drawn carriage she arrived in with her father; she put great effort into having everything turn out perfectly on her special day. Except for a few glitches (the wind knocking over a potted tree during the ceremony and being announced as the new "Mr. and Mrs." with her maiden name), the whole beautiful day went according to plan.

Everything had gone so smoothly we were surprised when my husband got a frantic phone call from my daughter the next morning. The young couple was at the airport waiting to leave on their honeymoon, and Emily was afraid they weren't going to let her board. She had made the flight reservations under what would be her new married name but didn't take into account the fact that she wouldn't yet have identification to prove it. Her driver's license was still under her maiden name, so she needed their marriage certificate to prove she was who she said she was. Fortunately, we hadn't left town yet, so my husband, who officiated at the wedding, drove to the airport with the marriage license, cleared up the misunderstanding, and the kids were off on their long-awaited honeymoon.

Have you struggled to walk in your identity? To prove to others you are who you say you are? It says in 2 Corinthians 5:17 that if we are in Christ we have new identities (the New International Version says we are "new creation[s]"). The New Living Translation tells us we become a new person, and the Amplified Bible tells us we get a fresh start. The old is gone. Everything is new and different. When we first enter into a relationship with Christ, this truth is obvious to us, but sometimes the longer we walk with Him, the more we take this for granted. Or perhaps we begin to listen to those old voices from our past trying to define us and tell us who we are. This is another lie we must defeat with His truth. We are *new*. Everything is different now. The old "us" has no power over us anymore.

Paul describes this age-old battle of the flesh versus the spirit in Romans 7. In chapter eight he tells us how Christ has won that battle for us, and we are already conquerors. Romans 8:1–2 (MSG) puts it this way:

> With the arrival of Jesus, the Messiah, that fateful dilemma is resolved. Those who enter into Christ's being-here-for-us no longer have to live under a continuous, low-lying black cloud. A new power is in operation. The Spirit of life in Christ, like a strong wind, has magnificently cleared the air, freeing you from a fated lifetime of brutal tyranny at the hands of sin and death.

According to Romans 5:5 and 15:13, and Acts 1:8, we have the power of the Holy Spirit within us. When we believe in Christ, we are marked with His seal (Ephesians 1:13), and our bodies are now the Holy Spirit's temple or home (1 Corinthians 6:19). Paul tells us in Philippians 4:13 he can do all things through Christ; Matthew 19:26 (NIV) tells us "with God all things are possible." What does all this mean? The Holy Spirit distributed our gifts (Hebrews 2:4) and empowers us to use them. God not only has created us and given us gifts, He has also given us the ability through His Spirit to use them for His purposes. You are uniquely gifted; you are strategically placed. God has called you to do His work using His talents with His power. In other words, you just have to be yielded to Him and let Him make all the effort! Can it really be that simple? In theory, yes. In practice—we still fight our old nature as Paul describes in Romans 7, but we don't need to get stuck there. Paul says in Romans 8:29–30 (NLT),

> For God knew his people in advance, and he chose them to become like his Son, so that his Son would be the firstborn among many brothers and sisters. And having chosen them, he called them to come to him. And having called them, he gave them right standing with himself. And having given them right standing, he gave them his glory.

We have everything we need to live out and walk in our giftedness—in our new identities. God has called you to this place, for this time, for this reason—to use your giftedness to help others.

Second Kings 5 tells the story of a young Israelite girl who is captured during a border raid and brought to Syria to be a handmaid to the wife of the army commander. Not much else is given to us about this young girl—not even her name. But we can imagine her circumstances and that life had not turned out exactly as she had expected. She was a servant, a slave, a captive—not words we would like to use to describe us. Her living situation had changed dramatically from what she knew before, yet in these few verses I think we can see that she knew her true identity. She was confident in her Jewish heritage, knew enough about who she was and where she was from to offer counsel from the wellspring of her knowledge of God and His prophet.

When she finds out that her master Naaman has leprosy, she speaks to his wife: "She said to her mistress, 'If only my master would see the prophet who is in Samaria! He would cure him of his leprosy' " (2 Kings 5:3 NIV). With only a few words she sets in motion an amazing chain of events. Naaman speaks to the King of Aram, who sends a letter to the King of Israel and then sets Naaman on a journey to see Elisha, the prophet of God in Israel. The rest of the chapter tells the story of how he eventually is healed and comes to believe in the one true God.

We can draw many lessons from these events, but I don't want to miss what started it all. One girl, who walked out her faith and spoke in obedience of what she knew to be true, helped change the course of not just one man's life but all those he came in contact with. Her sphere of influence was huge, even though society and her circumstances would not point to that. She could have easily thought, *Why bother? In the grand scheme of things I'm of no consequence. God doesn't even know I exist. I can't do anything for Him.*

Have you told yourself "I can't. . ." or "I'm not. . ."? God *is*! When we use whatever He has given us—however big or small we deem it to be—He can make amazing things happen. We often get this turned around in our thinking. We put more trust in our abilities than we do in the One who gave them to us.

A number of years ago my husband and I went on a mission trip to Nepal with a team from local churches. When we got in-country we found out that the group would be split into two smaller groups: one a medical team that would go out into the villages, while our team would focus more on teaching in the Bible schools and church plants. We also found out that because Nepal was a Hindu state, it was illegal to persuade people to change their religion. It seemed our plans for evangelistic outreach would be limited. We had just finished our first meal in a local restaurant, and as we headed back to our hotel our half of the team discussed this new information. We lamented this change in plans but decided that our focus would have to be on encouraging the believers at the various Bible schools we would be visiting.

With horns blaring and brakes squealing, bicycles, motorcycles, and taxis fought for the right-of-way on the road. The downtown streets of Kathmandu were teaming with people as we walked back to our hotel. As we passed the king's palace on one side of the road and beggars on the other side, a young Nepali man called Mohan approached us and asked us if we were Americans. We assured him we were. Then he asked if we were Christians and if we had a Bible. My husband told him that if he would follow us back to where we were staying, he would give him a Bible. Mohan agreed, and we settled down on our hotel terrace to talk with him. After explaining the plan of salvation to him we made plans to meet with him the next day, expecting him to want to think about the things we had just discussed. One of the men began to pray and Mohan interrupted him: "Wait, wait! You don't understand," he said. "I want to accept Jesus right now."

In our own fumbling attempt to do something for God, He showed us that He is the One who works. We thought our opportunities to witness for Him were limited because of man's laws and circumstances, but in fact we were the ones who were limiting God. It was nothing we did that drew Mohan to Him, nothing we said or shared of ourselves. He had heard a portion of God's Word before and was hungry for more and sought us out. God is the one who brought him to us; He is the one who transformed his heart. God did it all! It is the same no matter what our gifts are—without God in them they are worthless. Let me say that again: Whatever it is we do, *even if we do it well*, when we do it in our own strength we *fail*.

Jesus talked to His disciples about this in Mark 9. They had been traveling through Galilee and came to Capernaum. Along the way they were arguing, and Jesus asked them what they had been discussing. They think the One who knows everything has somehow missed that they've been arguing about which of them is the greatest! "He sat down, called the twelve disciples over to him, and said, 'Whoever wants to be first must take last place and be the servant of everyone else' " (Mark 9:35 NLT). Then He draws a little child into His arms and uses this illustration to set His disciples straight. It takes simple faith in Christ and dependence on Him alone. Proverbs 13:7 (NKJV) says,

"There is one who makes himself rich, yet has nothing; and one who makes himself poor, yet has great riches," or as *The Message* puts it, "A pretentious, showy life is an empty life; a plain and simple life is a full life." Isaiah 66:2 (NIV) says, "These are the ones I look on with favor: those who are humble and contrite in spirit, and who tremble at my word." Jeremiah 17:7 tells us that our confidence should be in Him, not in ourselves. Success by the world's standards (a favorable or desired outcome or an attainment of wealth, favor, or position) breeds confidence in ourselves, but those with confidence in God and His strength and abilities and not their own will be "like a tree planted by the water" (Jeremiah 17:8 NIV).

Second Peter 1:3 (NLT) tells us, "By his divine power, God has given us everything we need for living a godly life. We have received all of this by coming to know him, the one who called us to himself by means of his marvelous glory and excellence." We have everything we need, so what holds us back; what are we waiting for? Ephesians 4:24 (NIV) tells us "to put on the new self, created to be like God in true righteousness and holiness," and Colossians 3:10 (NLT) says, "Put on your new nature, and be renewed as you learn to know your Creator and become like him."

When we put on this new man, this new identity, we live out the life God intended for us. Romans 13:14 and Galatians 3:27 tell us to "put on" Christ. It says in 1 Corinthians 15:54 that we put on incorruption and immortality. Colossians 3:12–14 tells us to put on tender mercies, kindness, humility, meekness, longsuffering, and above all, to put on love. Now that's a brand-new wardrobe! When we settle for spiritual knockoffs, we settle for less than what God wants for us.

With over twenty years in pastoral ministry, my husband and I were well versed in what our lives should look like—what we thought was expected of us—both by God and our congregations. We knew all about the "should"; the problem was that in all of our *doing* what we should, we lost track of *being* what we should. Hurts, disappointments, and failed expectations all caved in on us. Instead of dealing with these issues head-on, we buried them under the pile of ongoing ministry pursuits and good deeds. In spite of the fact we were drowning in the emotion of past wounds and pain, we forged ahead, trying to live our lives in our own power. The result was not pretty. I stuffed anger, my husband stuffed pain, and when we couldn't hold any more of either the circumstances of our lives exploded all around us.

Have you ever been to the bottom of yourself— the place where you know you can do nothing to help yourself, make amends, or change your circumstances? For us, the first step was to confess our sin. Then, we needed to put off all of those cheap imitations we were wearing. We needed to exchange pride ("The LORD detests all the proud of heart." Proverbs 16:5 NIV) for humility ("God opposes the proud but shows favor to the humble." James 4:6 NIV), anger ("Human anger does not produce the righteousness that God desires." James 1:19–20 NIV) for self-control ("The fruit of the Spirit is love, joy, peace, forbearance, kindness, goodness, faithfulness, gentleness and self-control." Galatians 5:22–23 NIV), and efforts done in our own strength or "flesh" ("The Spirit gives life; the flesh counts for nothing." John 6:63 NIV) for the power of the Spirit ("Let the Holy Spirit guide your lives. Then you won't be doing what your sinful nature craves." Galatians 5:16–17 NLT). Galatians 6:8 states that if we sow to please the flesh, we will reap destruction, but when we sow to please the Spirit, we reap eternal life.

Galatians 3:3 (NLT) says "How foolish can you be? After starting your Christian lives in the Spirit, why are you now trying to become perfect by your own human effort?" Trying to live a spiritual life by our own efforts always ends in failure.

> *Those who live according to the flesh have their minds set on what the flesh desires; but those who live in accordance with the Spirit have their minds set on what the Spirit desires. The mind governed by the flesh is death, but the mind governed by the Spirit is life and peace. The mind governed by the flesh is hostile to God; it does not submit to God's law, nor can it do so. Those who are in the realm of the flesh cannot please God.* (Romans 8:5–8 NIV)

My husband and I lived in Pennsylvania for several years not very far from the Youghiogheny River, which is a white-water rafting destination. On one of the guided rafting trips we took, we stopped at a swimming hole along the way. Each swimmer jumped from the high rock into the deep water, floated downstream, and climbed back up to the top of the rock to do it again. A large, black Labrador retriever had come down the river with one of the kayakers. To our amazement, the dog jumped off the rock into the river and floated downstream, too! While we had life jackets to help keep us afloat, the dog had a rough time in the fast-moving water. I watched as my husband's head bobbed out of the water, and the dog came up right beside him. In order to keep his head out of the water the dog tried to climb up on my husband, his paws pushing my husband's head back under the water each time he surfaced. This is the visual I think of when I remember that period of time in our lives when everything seemed to fall apart. Overwhelmed by working a full-time job, being a mother of three teenage children, being a pastor's wife, and helping care for my elderly mother-in-law who lived in an apartment attached to our house, I felt like I was struggling just to keep my head above water.

My husband and I had given our lives to serve Christ. We loved Him and were committed to ministry, to trying to help others. Somewhere along the way, however, we lost sight of the fact that we needed *Him* to do this through us. When we tried to accomplish what was spiritual in our own flesh, we failed. By living in the flesh my husband and I were drawn into sin by our own desires. James 1:13–15 tells us that it is not God who tempts us, but it is by our own choice. It was our rebellion that gave birth to sin in our lives—and sin always brings about death. But God is in the business of defeating death! While our choices lead to anger, lies, adultery, and betrayal, God's forgiveness brings about redemption and reconciliation.

As my husband and I walked in repentance, we found that God's grace was more than enough to renew not only our personal spiritual lives but our marriage as well. We realized that we had chosen the wrong wardrobe! We were wearing selfishness and pride, discontent and complaint, wrong motives and unbelief. When we put these off and confessed our sin, were able to put on His righteousness (Ephesians 6:14) and His holiness (Ephesians 4:24). By His grace we were able to do in His Spirit what we were unable to do on our own—live the life He intended us to live.

My husband and I obtained our new identities the moment we each believed in Christ. God had given us everything we needed to live out our faith, but when we tried to do that without His power, we failed. It was only by giving up our own efforts that we found His strength to become who He created us to be—made in His image. According to 1 Peter 1:15–16, we are called to be holy because God is holy. But living a holy life can only be done in His power, not our own. Romans 12:9–19 in *The Message* gives us some pretty clear instructions of just how we should live out this new life we have:

Love from the center of who you are; don't fake it. Run for dear life from evil; hold on for dear life to good. Be good friends who love deeply; practice playing second fiddle. Don't burn out; keep yourselves fueled and aflame. Be alert servants of the Master, cheerfully expectant. Don't quit in hard times; pray all the harder. Help needy Christians;

*be inventive in hospitality. Bless your enemies; no
cursing under your breath. Laugh with your happy
friends when they're happy; share tears when
they're down. Get along with each other; don't be
stuck-up. Make friends with nobodies; don't be the
great somebody. Don't hit back; discover beauty
in everyone. If you've got it in you, get along with
everybody. Don't insist on getting even; that's not
for you to do. "I'll do the judging," says God. "I'll
take care of it."*

God takes care of it! The power to live this new life comes
from Him, from His Spirit living within us. If we just look
at this as a list of dos and don'ts it can be overwhelming
because frankly, we don't have the power on our own to
live this out. It takes Him living in us, and this is exactly
why He sent the Holy Spirit to help us. He is not only our
helper (John 14:16), but He also brings us rebirth and
renewal (Titus 3:5). He is our teacher (Luke 12:12), our
advocate (Romans 8:26), and so much more!

This lesson of knowing our true identity was a difficult-
but-oh-so-rewarding journey for my husband and me.
We no longer live trying to please others, or do what is
expected, or bury pain and hurts in our lives. Authentic
living has brought about true clarity in the way we look
at ourselves—and others. Because of God's grace and
mercy showered on us, we can more easily offer it to
others. We no longer try to live this spiritual life in our own
power but in His alone. We still fail. We still stumble. But
now instead of dusting ourselves off, we reach out our

hand to God and allow Him to pull us back up. There is a lot of freedom in admitting you can't do it on your own! It's not circumstances in our lives that have changed—it is how we look at them that has made the difference.

Gideon lived in the time of Judges over the nation of Israel. God had delivered them out of Egypt, and after rebellion and wandering in the desert, they entered the land God had promised to them. Joshua had taken over as their leader after Moses died, and while they had success in settling in the land, they failed in driving out all of God's enemies. We can follow the pattern of Israel's rebellion, sin, confession, and repentance that led to the arrogance of thinking they didn't need God's help, which only led to rebellion and sin again. During this period of history the Lord delivered the nation of Israel over to the hand of the Midianites. Their enemies had them on the run. Judges 6:1–2 describes how they had to hide in the mountains in caves and dens. Whatever they planted in crops and produced, the Midianites along with the Amalekites would come and destroy, leaving nothing for man or beast to eat. "Midian so impoverished the Israelites that they cried out to the Lord for help" (Judges 6:6 NIV). God finally had their attention!

Gideon was threshing wheat in secret in the winepress to hide it from the Midianites when the Lord sent an angel to him with a message, which was basically, "God is with you. Now go get 'em!" To which Gideon replied, "Who, me?" (That's my paraphrase, of course!) Gideon wants to know if God is with him, and with Israel, and asks where were the miracles and the wonders told about by his parents and grandparents?

Have you ever wondered, "Where are You, God?" God's reply to Gideon is found in Judges 6:14–16 (msg):

> But GOD faced him directly: "Go in this strength that is yours. Save Israel from Midian. Haven't I just sent you?" Gideon said to him, "Me, my master? How and with what could I ever save Israel? Look at me. My clan's the weakest in Manasseh and I'm the runt of the litter." GOD said to him, "I'll be with you. Believe me, you'll defeat Midian as one man."

Although he is fearful and seeks constant reassurance along the way, Gideon follows the Lord's instructions. He destroys the altars used to worship other gods. As the enemy gathers in retaliation, Gideon sends messengers throughout the land for the men of Israel to come and fight. Still, Gideon is wavering—is God really asking him to lead Israel in battle? God assures him that He is. There is a lesson to be learned here. Thirty-three thousand men gathered to fight, but God said that was too many because the people would claim the victory as their own and not God's. So God told Gideon to tell all those who were fearful to leave. Twenty-two thousand left and went home! But God said there were still too many. So Gideon took ten thousand men down to the water and told them to get a drink. Those who knelt down to drink were sent on home; the ones who lapped up the water with their tongue stayed to fight.

Gideon's army was down to three hundred—but God isn't finished making His point! Gideon and his men survey the Midianites, which are like "grains of sand on the seashore" (Judges 7:12 MSG). That night the Lord tells Gideon to go down and grasp the victory, but if Gideon has any doubts, then he should take his armor bearer and listen to the men in the enemy camp. Gideon overhears some men talking about a dream one of them had, and the other man interprets it as, "This has to be the sword of Gideon son of Joash, the Israelite! God has turned Midian—the whole camp!—over to him" (Judges 7:14 MSG). Gideon goes back to his men, and confident that the Lord is with them, he arms each man with a trumpet and an empty jar with a torch in it. He splits the army into three groups, and they surround the enemy, blow their trumpets, and shout as they break the jars from the torches. Thrown into chaos, the Midianites in their confusion began to kill one another. Terrified, the ones who survived took off running for their lives. Gideon then sends messengers out to recruit help, and the men from the tribe of Ephraim join the chase and soundly defeat the Midianites. Vastly outnumbered and with no weapons, the Israelites realize that when God is on their side, He is all they need.

God is all we need. Do you believe it? And more importantly, are you living like you believe it? Gideon was a man who had doubts, but God in His graciousness assured him again and again. If you are wondering if God is working in your life—ask Him! He will answer and bring reassurance. The Israelites went through a cycle similar to what many of us today go through. Ignoring the truth that God has already given us, we try things our way, which leads to sin and rebellion. When life crashes in on us we become desperate for His help. God offers forgiveness, which we gratefully accept, then life moves forward and things go pretty well for us, until we decide to follow our own path again instead of God's—and the cycle begins all over again. We can break that cycle of sin in our lives by choosing to stop trying to do it on our own.

It comes down to a choice—doing life our way or God's way. When we choose God's way, we allow Him to work in and through us instead of relying on our own strength and abilities—abilities that we received from Him!

Discussion Questions

1. Read 2 Timothy 1:9. God has called us to live a holy life. Do you find this difficult? Why or why not? ....
   ....
   ....

2. Do you struggle with feeling you are unable to accomplish certain tasks? Name any areas you might be struggling in. Now write out Philippians 4:13. How does this verse change the way you view yourself?
   ....
   ....

3. Read Proverbs 16:3. What is the first step in making sure your plans succeed? ....
   ....
   ....

4. The letter to Philemon is a letter the apostle Paul wrote to his coworker. What does he pray for Philemon in verse 6? ....
   ....
   ....

5. Galatians 5:16 tells us to walk in the Spirit and Ephesians 5:18 tells us to be filled with the Spirit. Fill in the following blanks describing what else we are to be filled with:

Philippians 1:11..

....

Psalm 71:8 ....

....

Romans 15:14..

....

1 Peter 1:8...

....

John 17:13 ....

....

Colossians 1:9...

....

6. How does 1 John 5:1–5 describe those who love God?

....

....

7. According to James 1:4, what is the result if we allow God to work through our circumstances?.....................
....
....

8. Read 2 Corinthians 3:4–5. What is our confidence in? Where does our sufficiency and competence come from?...
....
....

Notes

CHAPTER SIX
Transformed to Trust

*For God has not given us a spirit of fear,
but of power and of love and of a sound
mind.*

2 TIMOTHY 1:7 NKJV

$\mathcal{I}$ stood on the mountainside of Petra, the ancient city in the Middle Eastern country of Jordan. All around me towered the beautiful, red-tinted mountains that comprised the walls of security for this ancient city. Spectacular architecture lined the sides of these mountains; man-made homes, temples, and water channels were carved into rock. The age-old ruins of pillars and gates jutted into the air—it was breathtaking. As I scanned the scenery below, a dusty and winding "road" snaked its way through the city, camels plodded through the sand, and Arab women blanketed in black burkas sat selling their trinkets. There was no mistaking I was in the Middle East, and it was beautiful.

As I drank in the sights, I thought back to all our group had experienced on this trip. We had the privilege of meeting and spending time with our brothers and sisters in Christ, people I had never met before but connected with on a deeper level because of Jesus. Listening, laughing, sharing, and celebrating changed lives—our time together had been only a God-thing. Relationships within our own group had blossomed, and I was able to gaze upon places I've only read about in God's Word. And to think, I could have missed it all.

Satan has used fear in my life as a war tactic for as long as I can remember. From the fear of making a mistake to the fear of what people thought, I could worry with the best of them. God has grown me in a lot of ways through the years, but this root of fear was buried deep. So, when I received a call several years ago from the missions director at my church asking if I wanted to go to the Middle East, well, that was something I needed to pray about and process. Knowing what I've seen on television and read in the news, traveling to the Middle East and flying over the Atlantic Ocean to boot didn't exactly set this woman at peace. However, God had something in mind. Peace came, and I accepted the invitation.

As fall approached and the departure day drew near, I began to experience an unsettling feeling—or you could call it more like panic. People who heard I would be traveling overseas began offering their opinions, thinking in some way it was helpful: "Well, I hope what happened to that missionary doesn't happen to you." I always received the same puzzled look with the common question, "Why in the world are you going *there*?" But my favorite was, "Well, I hope you come back." Umm . . .really? Yeah, it would be great if that worked into the plans! I had a husband and three sons, and little did they know that it was that very thought that flooded my mind: *What if I don't come back?*

As if those little seeds of doubt weren't enough, I had been receiving daily devotions online, and apparently a new series had started. Lo and behold, it was all about death. By this time, I was convinced I was going to die. Now, as normal as the fear to travel into a war zone may have been initially, Satan continued to blow it bigger in my mind and soul until it became crippling. That's what Satan does—he makes fear so big that it fills our perspective, and we can't see God anymore. Using fear, Satan tried to distract and destroy. But God stepped in and trumped Satan's tactic. God used that fear as a stepping-stone to my surrender and increased my faith in who He was. As I prayed, the pervading thought that continued to come to my mind was, *Will you trust Me?*

I left with my group that day really not knowing if I was going to come back or not. In those short but ever so intense months, God had taken me on a faith journey of incredible proportions, and I hadn't even stepped on the plane. Don't think I was confident, because I wasn't. I was scared stiff. He knew that and held my hand the whole way. He had led me to a place where all I knew was that I could trust Him, no matter what my plane ride held or the perceived danger of traveling in foreign lands. I knew He was my Safe Place.

So as I stood staring at the majesty of His mountains overlooking Petra and thought about all that God had done in the lives of His people, hot tears flowed down my face. I didn't hear His voice audibly, but it was like a "knowing" that came over me. In that moment of drinking in the magnificence of His creation, I knew God was huge. I knew He was bigger than *all* things, including the fear that had attempted to keep me at home and the perspective and opinions of man. I knew that His plans for His children reflected the immensity and the expanse of the scenery before me. While this sense of His magnificence held me, I knew in my spirit like never before that He can be trusted. The blind faith He had given me to step on the plane, He confirmed here. No matter what or whom we face, God can be trusted. He's always bigger, His ways are always better, His words are always true, and He loves us far beyond what we can think or imagine.

The potential for fear is everywhere—fear of heights, public speaking, flying, the future, financial loss, failing, confrontation, rejection, disease. But one of the most damaging and deadly fears we deal with is the fear of man. I came home one evening, put my coat and purse down, and noticed the light blinking on my answering machine. Pushing PLAY I heard the same voice we had heard numerous times before. A woman from the community would leave us messages, criticizing various people we knew. She would often call them names or tell us of their devious schemes. Sometimes she would give a cackle and then hang up. This night, she left a message for me—*about* me. And it wasn't nice. My sons laughed so hard, they recorded it. And they certainly enjoyed playing it over and over. It was nothing I allowed to sit in my heart because it was rather comical, but I have to admit, it stung when I first heard it.

It's not the first time I have been criticized, and I'm sure it won't be the last. I have received criticism that has been well deserved and some that has been more interesting, like being "too kind." I had a friend who encouraged me to slow down because I was too busy, and when I did she looked at me and asked, "So, what are you going to do with yourself now?" Some comments

I have looked at and worked at changing my ways of doing things, others I have just shook my head at. Still other comments of disapproval have debilitated me for days. I'm sure some of you can relate. The fact is, we will never be able to please all those who are watching. The good news is, we weren't made to. The unfortunate thing is, we try anyway.

Our natural bent includes the longing to be accepted, but instead of looking to the One who stands with open arms to meet that need, our eyes land on those we do life with—those who are not capable of fully giving us what we ultimately desire. We want to attain man's approval, and sometimes we find ourselves jumping through hoops to gain it before we even know what hit us. I have listened to women whose marriages have been affected and divided over a desire to please parents. I have observed young women hesitate to dress femininely because their parents expressed openly their desire for a son. I have watched teens starve their bodies because they want to be seen by others as "beautiful." I have watched anxiety steal peace from heart after heart because we've answered to the wrong name. We will alter our choices and behavior, forfeit wisdom and "the best," in order to become what others want us to be. In doing so, we have forfeited the beauty, the confidence, and the joy of being the one God made us to be. We have failed to wear and live in the identity Jesus died to give us—His identity.

I listened to her struggle—this gifted, beautiful "inside and out" woman of God—as she described her heart's desire to be approved of by one of her friends.

It consumed her thinking, her behavior, and even her choice of wardrobe. She was trapped and miserable. Tears welled up in my eyes as I listened to her, thinking how sad God must be as He watches His daughters strive to please those whose perspectives are dark. We allow our longing to be accepted and approved to control us in hopes of hearing that one comment of praise, that one statement of affirmation, which will feed the monster of fear living in our hearts. It's called people-pleasing, and it can rob the joy right out from under us.

You know what I'm talking about. You can work hard, and the meeting, event, or party you've planned goes off without a hitch. You can receive lots of positive feedback, but there's that one negative comment that you just can't shake. And that's where your focus stays. You know what it's like to make decisions solely based on what others want you to do despite what you think. If you make a decision displeasing to another, you may second-guess yourself. You won't tell someone the truth or be transparent because you fear his or her response. You care what people think of you and have found yourself subconsciously looking to others for your value and worth. Who you thought you were one day changes the next depending on the mood or opinions of your coworkers, family members, and friends. With their approval of your performance came acceptance, but now with their disapproval, comes rejection. Talk about an identity crisis! This can go on for years, until one day you find yourself miserable, owned by anxiety, and downright weary. That's because fear will suck the life and passion out of you. But because of Jesus, we can know who we are every single minute of the day no matter what mood others or we ourselves are experiencing.

We can take off the knockoff identity of *people-pleaser* that's rooted in fear, because when we began a new life in Christ, He clothed us in security, acceptance, and approval. When God looked at His Son He said, "This is my Son, whom I love; with him I am well pleased" (Matthew 3:17 NIV). As believers, we are hidden in Jesus (Colossians 3:3). If we are living in Him, what does that make us? Pleasing. Scripture says, "It's impossible to please God apart from faith. And why? Because anyone who wants to approach God must believe both that he exists and that he cares enough to respond to those who seek him" (Hebrews 11:6 MSG). You are pleasing to God our Father, because of Jesus. Because of faith in and dependence on Jesus, our hearts have shifted, our purpose has changed, and our focus is different. Our goal is not to keep our ears tuned to the opinion of the crowd but to keep our ears, our eyes, our hearts, and our lives focused on the One who speaks truth. And then believe Him.

Have you ever watched an animal that was trapped? I'm an animal lover so when I saw this once, I never forgot it. Pacing back and forth, it bites at all sides of its cage looking for any way to escape. It may find itself in a snare, with a nooselike cable around its neck. It may find itself in a leg hold, pulling and biting at the trap trying to free itself. As unappealing as it sounds, unless it chews its leg off, it usually means the end.

The day I sat across from my friend and listened to

her struggle for approval, Proverbs 29:25 came to mind: "Fear of man will prove to be a snare, but whoever trusts in the LORD is kept safe" (NIV). Fear is not only an emotion that can show up when something scares us, but it also produces consternation and anxiety. Consternation is that fear or panic that leads to utter and total confusion, much like the animal experiences in the grips of the snare. When we are steeped in fear of man we can't see clearly. We can't think clearly. Rather than go forward, we think and rethink the situation, becoming more anxious. Our mode becomes survival, and we're led by emotion. We're confused; we may feel desperate, and peace continues to elude us. It's not a life-giving combination for any of us. Rather than resting in the security and truth of Jesus, we're living in the fear of man.

But when we trust in the Lord, scripture says we are kept safe. The word "safe" here refers to being inaccessible or set up high. Jesus is our example time and time again when He was faced with the expectations of man. His heartbeat was not to please man and gain his approval (John 2:25; 5:41) but to trust and obey His Father, carrying out the work that He was given to do. He spoke the words of His Father no matter if it offended people or not (Matthew 15:10–14; Mark 10:17–23) and upheld God's way over man's traditions. And He didn't fret over it one single time. As important as people were to Him, His relationship with His Father took precedence.

He was criticized, rejected, spit upon, and despised. He was continually being misrepresented and misunderstood. He was accused repeatedly of evil or impure motives. But He didn't stop trusting His Father no matter how hard, frightening, or discouraging the situation. Being fully God but also fully man, He needed to return to His Father and His identity over and over again. But no matter what man did to Him, He ultimately remained inaccessible in the hands of His Father. Too many times, we have become ensnared, distracted, and hindered by fear. We can experience changed thinking and living, peace and security when we stop trying to manufacture our own security in people's acceptance and trust Jesus in His.

Trusting God is taking our eyes off fear and putting them on His Son. Jesus, our Prince of Peace (Isaiah 9:6), has come to give us peace of mind, heart, and spirit (John 14:27). He promises that when we come to Him, He comes near to us (James 4:8), that He is our strong tower and when we run to Him, we are safe (Proverbs 18:10; Psalm 34:4). He wants us to give Him whatever is on our hearts, our concerns, anxieties, and fears, because He cares for us (1 Peter 5:7). Fear is bound to come into our lives, but I've heard it said in order to overcome fear, we "do it afraid" a little bit at a time while trusting God every step of the way. Fear doesn't have to paralyze or rule us anymore. In the face of fear, we can profess our trust, believe God, and walk forward. We can talk to Him, focus on giving Him gratitude or praise. Reading His promises, repeating His truth to ourselves (including our identity in Christ) throughout the day, or remembering His goodness and what He has done in our lives, all resets our perspective. Trusting is returning to truth; it's returning to Jesus. We are reminded of who He is and that it is His Holy Spirit that lives in and through us.

We have been given a spirit of power—Jesus and His Gospel message (Romans 1:16–17; 1 Corinthians 1:18, 24). His arrival on earth brought us a certain hope. His death gave us His righteous and spotless record, His resurrection abundant and eternal life. We are forgiven, acceptable, seen as perfect and complete in Christ. His judgment and wrath for our sin has been poured on His Son. There is no more wrath for us to bear. We can know that God's power that raised Jesus from the dead is the same power working in us today (Ephesians 1:18–20). So to live in His power is to rest in Jesus—choosing, believing, and depending on Him and walking in the identity He gave us. So when we are afraid of being rejected by others, He accepts us. When we are afraid of circumstances, we are secure in Him. When we are afraid we can't measure up, He already has. You see, our identity is all about Jesus. So can you imagine what God can do in and through us with fear out of the driver's seat and His power in charge? God's glory is revealed. People are set free. The Kingdom of God spreads. Do you see why our realization and embracing of our identity *in* Christ is dangerous to the devil but life changing for us and for the world around us? Do you understand why God would jump for joy when we begin to understand who we are in Him (Luke 10:17–21) and what He has done for us? We can know and believe that God's purposes and plans will prevail (Proverbs 21:30). He may not choose to change our situation, but His Spirit of comfort, courage, and power will certainly change us and our response in the face of fear.

> *I, even I, am he who comforts you. Who are you*
> *that you fear mere mortals, human beings who*
> *are but grass, that you forget the LORD your Maker,*
> *who stretches out the heavens and who lays the*
> *foundations of the earth. . . . For I am the LORD your*
> *God, who stirs up the sea so that its waves roar—*
> *the LORD Almighty is his name. I have put my words*
> *in your mouth and covered you with the shadow of*
> *my hand—I who set the heavens in place, who laid*
> *the foundations of the earth, and who say to Zion,*
> *"You are my people."* (Isaiah 51:12–13, 15–16 NIV)

When we fear man, we forget God. We make others big and Him small. We make their standard higher than His. The good news is we don't have to fight for man's approval anymore, because we already have God's. Jesus Christ is God's approval and praise (John 5:44)! Gaining God's approval and praise is receiving this gift of grace named Jesus.

So how do we handle and interpret criticism that comes our way? Above all, we need to remember our identity in Christ as we process the words and messages of others. Words can be hurtful because so often people are speaking from their own woundedness and fear issues. (We need to stop here and apply this to our lives as the "speaker." As casually as we throw out words, we need to remember that our words have meaning. We are wise to be aware of the place we speak from and the issues that we struggle with that would fuel the fire beneath our words. We need to remember who we are speaking to—God's beloved.) However, there is nothing anyone can say to us that will change or remove our identity in Christ. We are pleasing and complete in Him (Colossians 2:10).

Our job is to take the criticism to the Lord and interpret it through Him. We can trust Him with our hearts. God is full of mercy. He is gentle and humble, and His heart is for us. We can ask Him if there is truth in this criticism from which we can learn and grow. If so, God will show us, and He will do it with kindness and gentleness, never with condemnation or shame. We also can take those criticisms and approach trusted and God-loving individuals who will help us process the words and tell us the truth. Not just those people who will agree with us but who can be objective and who love God, walk in His transforming grace, know His Word, and have our best interests at heart. When we are in the midst of situations where our view is clouded, it is essential we have God-centered relationships and an objective party who can help us see truth in order to step out of the snare. Seeing truth may mean bringing our overinflated sense of fear into check or realizing someone's criticism is not founded. If criticism is untrue, our job is to dismiss it. Why dwell on things that aren't true, that steal our energy and joy (Philippians 4:4–8)?

Choosing to trust God and let go of pleasing man may be difficult. We have been operating in one system for a long time, so finding our footing on a new foundation may feel unsettling. But remember, as Christ-followers we're not operating in a system anymore; we're living in a relationship with Jesus. Trusting God rather than fearing man may mean making decisions that aren't considered "normal." It may mean slowing your pace and laying things down to make room for God to orchestrate His opportunities in your life. It may mean letting things go that drained your desire and passion rather than doing more in order to please others. That may mean disappointing people because you stop living to meet their expectations. That may mean coming to the realization and acceptance that the words of affirmation you long for from man won't come, and you're okay with that because your heart has shifted. It may mean listening to people's disapproving comments and learning to discern what is or isn't truth, what we could have done better, and what we would do over again.

A friend of mine, who is active in women's ministry at her church and openly admits she is a people-pleaser, shared with me her struggle with a few negative comments surrounding a Bible study she was leading. She couldn't dismiss them from her mind even though she saw God moving and working in the lives of various women. Simultaneously, she was experiencing negative feedback from people concerning another situation in her life. Needless to say, she was growing discouraged by the barrage of criticism. After encouraging her to examine it for truth, I pointed out the fact that because she's a people-pleaser, God may be using this to allow her the opportunity to grow through it. Instead of bowing at the altar of the fear of man and bearing the weight of others' expectations, why not use this opportunity to choose to walk in her Father's pleasure? Why not focus on what He has called her to? Are her heart's motives pure? Is she doing it for His honor and glory? If not, then talk to Him about it; confess it and change direction. But if so, then walk in His pleasure.

We do what we do for an audience of One. If it is pleasing to Him, then does it matter if Betty and Wilma aren't pleased? If others are making decisions pleasing to Him, does it matter if you and I aren't pleased? Trusting God may mean hearing people's disapproval but choosing to love them and forging ahead with God's plan. Trusting God usually means stepping out in faith and feeling completely vulnerable.

Several years ago, my husband sensed God urging him to resign from his job. He obeyed and turned in his resignation, but for various reasons his three-month notice turned into seven due to the needs at his job. This was not your normal situation as resignations go. My husband had nothing lined up—there was no job in mind that was next. He knew God had laid it on his heart, and he obeyed. When he first told me I was surprised to say the least. I knew that God was stirring something in his heart, that his time at this current job was coming to a close, but I didn't know when. So, when he told me, I went into fear mode instantly. Tears rolled down my cheeks immediately thinking of the upcoming tonsillectomy for one of our children. How will we pay for it? What about insurance?

It was then that God stepped into my thoughts as Bruce explained how God had moved in his heart earlier that evening, prompting the resignation. After I listened, the words out of my mouth were, "I'm just going to have to trust God in you." We prayed and peace fell over me.

A month rolled by and there was nothing in the way of job possibilities. We engaged in talks with some people but found only closed doors. Another month went by and several opportunities came. We prayed about them, but God's peace wasn't there, so we continued to wait. Another month, then another, more opportunities, no peace. When Bruce resigned, we shared with our sons what God was asking us to do and that we as a family were in for a journey of faith. We told them we knew we would see God move in miraculous ways. Let me tell you—God didn't let us down. There were days I would be unsettled and Bruce would be peaceful and strong. There were days when he would look at me and wonder if he had heard right. God would speak through me with confident resolve and reassurance. It was amazing, but we never had days when we both questioned at the same time. God had us right where He wanted us—dependent on Him.

Throughout these months we heard lots of talk from people. We heard we were nuts, the decision was crazy (and it's true, it's not your typical behavior), people were angry with us, and we even heard rumors about what we were going to do next and our motives for doing it. I remember one individual pulling my husband to the corner of the room, chuckling and asking him, "Okay, now what are you *really* going to do? What's your plan?" My husband responded, "I really don't know." She punched him in the arm kiddingly and laughed, "Yes, you do. You're no fool." He and I looked at each other and just smiled.

Finally, October came, and I remember asking Bruce what we were going to do about health benefits with three young boys. With a smile, he joked, "Well, the boys just can't get sick next year." I wasn't humored, so he resorted to the old cliché, "God will provide." The next day, there was a knock at my front door. A friend and businesswoman had stopped in to make me an offer, a job with health benefits. Not only that, but it was a job that afforded me the opportunity to continue to serve women through mentoring, speaking, and writing. It turns out, "God will provide" wasn't merely a cliché after all. We marveled at God's faithfulness. Not only that, but God had placed on Bruce's heart the reality of Marketplace Ministry, something he had dreamed of doing one day. People were supportive, saw the vision and the need, so we stood back and watched God put it into motion.

December was Bruce's last month working, and God had waited until the end of November to reveal His divine plan to us. For the last two years, we have watched God put marriages back together; save lives; grow people in leadership, faith, and character; and lead people through the storms of life to safety. The power of His Word and Spirit is bearing fruit not only in the hearts of these men and women but also in their families and those they serve. God has blessed us above and beyond. He is our Leader, Protector, Provider, Defender, Power, our very

Life. He has allowed us to have a "window seat" as He moves and works in hearts and lives. He did something we could never have made happen, and our sons were able to witness it all. He is limitless! He is trustworthy. To a woman who wrestles with people-pleasing, to a man who holds as one of his top priorities providing for his family, God's message to us was, "Will you trust Me?"

Oftentimes God will test us where the fear looms largest. God looks at you and me and says, "I have some of you, but I want all of you." In Matthew 16, Jesus takes His disciples to the most pagan city in Judea, Caesarea Philippi. It was in this region where the fertility god, Pan, was worshipped. Not only was he a false god, but he also was disgusting and vile. At the foot of the mountain was a cave, and enclosing this cave was Pan's temple. The gates to this temple were termed "the gates of hell." Horrific acts of evil, including child sacrifice, encompassed worship.[1] No respectable Jew would go there. But that didn't stop Jesus. It was here where Jesus stood with His disciples, facing the temple, to give them one of the most powerful object lessons they would ever receive. After Peter's profession of Jesus being the Christ, the Son of the living God, Jesus responds, "And I tell you that you are Peter, and on this rock I will build my church, and the gates of Hades will not overcome it" (Matthew 16:18 NIV). Jesus declares to His disciples, these mere men who will be entrusted to spread His Gospel message, that He will build His church in the most evil, most vile and frightening place

---

1. *http://www.generationword.com/Israel/caesarea_philippi.htm* (accessed January 7, 2012).

on earth, and evil will not stop Him. His church will grow; His message will spread. He will prevail.

My friend, as dark and daunting as fear may seem to us, it is powerless against our Mighty Savior. He is leading us through life and sometimes into scary places where no one really wants to go, facing the fears that we have avoided for so long. But with the Holy Spirit living within us, His identity upon us, and our lives hidden in Him, we don't have to be ruled by fear anymore. We have been transformed to trust Him because Christ is our courage, our strength, our very life (Colossians 3:3–4) for eternity and in our every day. Choose faith. Believe Him. Let Him lead the way, and watch Him do the incredible.

Discussion Questions

1. What fear do you find yourself wrestling with?..............
....
....

2. How have you struggled with people-pleasing? How can you relate to Proverbs 29:25? ....
....
....

3. Where do you find your focus when you are struggling with fear? Read the following scriptures: Joshua 1:6–9; 1 Kings 19:1–18; Psalm 23; Isaiah 40:11; Isaiah 41:10; Philippians 4:4–9; and 1 John 4:13–18. How do these verses speak to you? ....
....
....

4. Discuss this statement based on scripture: When we fear man, we forget God. How can you see this in your life? ....
....
....

5. Proverbs 8:35 (GNT), "Those who find me find life, and the Lord will be pleased with them." (The Book) ". . . whoever finds me finds life and wins approval from the Lord." How does it impact you to know that you are pleasing to God because of Jesus' gift of grace and identity? ....
....
....

6. What does it mean to you to know that receiving God's approval is receiving Jesus? ....
....
....

7. How do you handle criticism? How does the discussion about receiving criticism make you think about how you express it to others? ....
....
....

8. How have you stepped out in faith when God asked you to? What did you learn through your experience?
....
....

9. Is there an area in your life God doesn't have? How is He telling you that He has some of you but wants all of you? How is He asking you to trust Him? ....
....

Notes

....
....
....
....
....
....
....
....
....
....
....
....
....
....
....
....
....
....
....
....
....
....
....

Conclusion

Our identity in Christ gives us many new names, but "Loved" is the foundation of them all. In Luke 15 we read about our Father and His love for us. Henri Nouwen in *The Return of the Prodigal* speaks of God as a Father who watches for us, pursues us, and perseveres until He finds us.[1] He holds a love for us that isn't careful or stringent but a wild, let-go-of-all-dignity-and-run-to-us kind of love, a love that opens its arms, gathers us up, and swings us around in joy and laughter. It's a love that celebrates when we come home, where we're wrapped in the embrace of our Father, engulfed in His forgiveness, generosity, compassion, and approval.

His love doesn't depend on our behavior, our vocation, our awards, or our failures. He just wants us in His arms because we belong there. It's in these arms where we find all that we need and the "clothes of privilege" that come along with being His (v. 22). It's here where we find confidence, security, purpose, acceptance, worth, courage, and life-giving perspective. Everything He has, He generously and joyfully shares with us (vv. 31–32). So whether we've acted like the younger son leaving Him and searching elsewhere for the love we've always desired, or we've served Him dutifully for years like the older son and altogether missed the joy and meaning of being His—He

---

1. Henri J.M. Nouwen, *The Return of the Prodigal Son: A Story of Homecoming* (New York: Doubleday, 1992), 102.

invites us to run into His arms and experience true love and acceptance.

In his book, Nouwen asks a powerful and heart-prodding question: Will we dare to be loved as our Father longs to love us or insist on being loved as we feel we ought to be loved? Too often, like the older son in the story of the Prodigal, we allow our identity to be defined by what we do and the visible results or how we feel about things. When things change—whether a job, a season of life, or children leaving home—we flounder a little emotionally. *What will happen to me? Will I be successful? Will I have value in this new season?* And we catch ourselves defining ourselves by our activity. Here's some freeing news: God is far more interested in who we are than in what we do. In other words, it's more the "who" than the "do" that matters. To simply "be"—to allow Him to love us right where we are and find fulfillment—is learning to live in our identity in Christ.

Have you ever looked at your sons or daughters and caught a glimpse of what they looked like as little ones? It's a precious moment because we're taken back to a memory of what once was. But when God looks at us, He doesn't see us for what we were. He sees us for what we will become. Even though a little child learns, grows, matures, and changes, his name doesn't. As God's child, we've got an identity that is unchangeable. But we will continue to learn and grow, becoming the women God has called us to be, and He will never grow tired or impatient with us. He promises that His Holy Spirit will continue to work in us, and our resemblance to Jesus will be ever-increasing (2 Corinthians 3:18). It is by His grace that we are becoming who we already are—"For by one sacrifice he has made perfect forever those who are being made holy" (Hebrews 10:14 NIV). We don't have to pretend anymore, defend ourselves, prove ourselves, be somebody we're not, or wear a knockoff identity. Living in His embrace empowers us to be exactly who He made us to be. . .His beloved, simply and marvelously His.

Your identity can change today from hopeless to one overflowing with hope, from being weary to learning what it means to rest. You are no longer rejected but can experience what it is to be accepted and approved. You can be empowered to stop walking in defeat and discouragement and know victory because of Jesus. You no longer have to feel dead inside but can experience true life! Your life can change; Jesus is offering you a new beginning with Him. God is pursuing you, He loves you, and wants you as His own. He longs to bless you, to hold you, to show you Himself in a personal relationship. All you have to do is allow Him to do so. He is offering you the gift of His Son. Jesus died for you, rose again, and has not only saved you from your sin and from eternal separation from Him but will give you His Holy Spirit to live in you and give you abundant life through Him. He asks you to receive Him and believe Him, confessing Jesus as your Lord (Romans 10:9–13). His arms are open wide. . .

Jesus, I confess You as Lord of all. I believe that

You died on the cross, rose from the dead, and rescued me, a sinner. I know that there is nothing I can do to save myself; it is only through the gift of Your grace, through Jesus Christ. I receive the forgiveness You freely give me and thank You for washing away my sins. I ask for and receive Your Holy Spirit that You send to live within me. Thank You that You will guide me and teach me, that You will live through me. Thank You for the unchangeable, irrevocable, genuine identity You have given me. Thank You for who I am in You! In Jesus' name, amen.

Notes:

....
....
....
....
....
....
....
....
....
....
....
....
....
....
....
....
....
....
....
....
....
....
....
....
....

About the Authors

Jocelyn Hamsher lives in Sugarcreek, Ohio, with her husband and three sons. She is a speaker, mentor, author, and certified biblical counselor. Jocelyn has written *Do These Jeans Make Me Look Fat? Breaking the Cultural Mirror* (Barbour Publishing) and is a contributing author in the Circle of Friends devotional series.

Missy Horsfall, a pastor's wife for more than twenty years, is a Bible study teacher, board member, and speaker for Circle of Friends Ministries. She has been published in magazine and greeting card media. Missy is also executive producer and radio host for COF Ministries. She and her husband live in Ohio and have three married children and two adorable granddaughters.

What Is Circle of Friends?

Circle of Friends Ministries Inc. (COF) is a nonprofit organization established to build a pathway for women to come into a personal relationship with Jesus Christ and to build Christian unity among women. Our mission is to honor Jesus Christ through meeting the needs of women in our local, national, and international communities. Our vision is to be women who are committed to Jesus Christ, obediently seeking God's will, and fulfilling our life mission as Christ-followers. As individuals and as a corporate group, we minister a Christ-centered hope, biblically based encouragement, and unconditional love by offering God-honoring, Word-based teaching, worship, accountability, and fellowship to women in a nondenominational environment through speaker services, worship teams, daily web blogs and devotionals, radio programs, and GirlFriends teen events.

COF also partners with churches and women's groups to bring conferences, retreats, Bible studies, concerts, simulcasts, and servant evangelism projects to their communities. We have a Marketplace Ministry that teaches kingdom principles in the workplace and are committed to undergirding, with prayer and financial support, foreign mission projects that impact the world for Jesus Christ. Our goal is to evangelize the lost and edify the Body of Christ by touching the lives of women—locally, nationally, and globally. For more information, visit www.ourcircleoffriends.org.